SIMON & SCHUSTER MEGA CROSSWORD PUZZLE BOOK

Series 4

300 never-before-published crosswords

Edited by John M. Samson

GALLERY BOOKS

New York   London   Toronto   Sydney   New Delhi

G

Gallery Books
An Imprint of Simon & Schuster, Inc.
1230 Avenue of the Americas
New York, NY 10020

This Gallery Books trade paperback edition March 2020

GALLERY BOOKS and colophon are registered trademarks of Simon &
Schuster, Inc.

For information about special discounts for bulk purchases,
please contact Simon & Schuster Special Sales at 1-866-506-1949 or
business@simonandschuster.com.

The Simon & Schuster Speakers Bureau can bring authors to your live event.
For more information or to book an event, contact the Simon & Schuster
Speakers Bureau at 1-866-248-3049 or visit our website at
www.simonspeakers.com.

Designed by Sam Bellotto Jr.

Manufactured in the United States of America

20   19   18   17

ISBN 978-1-4165-8781-1

COMPLETE ANSWERS WILL BE FOUND AT THE BACK.

FOREWORD

RING THING   by Harvey Estes

(Letters in circles are an anagram of the riddle answer.)

ACROSS

1 Put a worm on
5 Confidence
7 Pull-off
9 **Start of a riddle**
11 Abounds
12 Type of flare or panel
14 Small shoulders?
15 Austerity
17 Do a double take
18 Police
20 Hendrix hairdo
21 White wader
23 **More of riddle**
24 **More of riddle**
25 VCR?
27 "I before E, except after C," e.g.
28 You guys of Arabia?
30 33 Across and others
31 Family nicknames
33 Exodus memorial
34 PC support
36 Sheltered bays
37 **End of riddle**
40 Give lip service?
41 They tell you where to go
42 Change for a fin

DOWN

1 Trumps
2 Play opening
3 Levin with a nest egg?
4 Contract conditions
5 Clothes lines
6 "Coffee, ___ Me?"
7 Butler on screen
8 Ignore the cue cards
9 Friends cross it
10 Top scout
11 Eagerly unwrap
13 Duffer on a golf cart?
14 Cover some of the cost of
16 Sends another way
17 Whole slew
19 Bear
22 Els pegs
26 Get Mad again
29 Mexican munchy
30 Variety show
32 "___ Lady" (Tom Jones song)
33 Covers with carbon
35 Holy beginning
36 Lobster features
38 Go round the bend
39 Sea peril

The Margaret Award winner is RARE WORDS I & II by Arthur S. Verdesca

JOHN M. SAMSON

1 WALK AROUND THE BLOCK   by Elizabeth C. Gorski

A pleasant stroll that starts at 1 Across and ends at 1 Down.

ACROSS

1 Cookie cutter?
6 Water carrier
10 "Quantum of Solace" hero
14 Father of the Dionne quintuplets
15 Violist's clef
16 "Gem City" of Pennsylvania
17 Osteopath's concern
18 Clean freak's nightmare
19 "P.S. I Love You" actress Gershon
20 Titanic letters
21 Alternate TITLE (with 57-A)
23 Matured
24 Thai cash
26 "Don't give up!"
27 Tribe of Delaware
29 "Musicophilia" author Sachs
31 Have shingles
32 Chinese dialect
33 The Karnali flows there
34 Like some divorces
36 NYC subway line
37 THEME (with "Side")
39 B. Obama, for one
42 Contaminate
43 Gloria Stivic's mom
48 Pay ending
49 Correlatives
50 Iterate
51 Ain't, in the past?
53 God, in Roma
55 Boyfriend
56 Washington nine
57 See 21 Across
60 Capp and Pacino
61 "What's ___ for me?"
62 Solves kakuro puzzles
63 Henpeck
65 Fate who spins the thread of life
66 Swarm
67 Vernel Bagneris musical "___ Time"
68 Eats
69 Effortless
70 It holds water

DOWN

1 Mint julep ingredient
2 Like "The Full Monty" strippers
3 Close connection
4 "Fields of Gold" singer Cassidy
5 Creek at the Masters
6 Conductor Kurt
7 Quell
8 "Like ___ not!"
9 Al Gore, for one
10 Got cracking
11 Paper tiger?
12 Spare part?
13 Like a job with no future
22 District: Abbr.
25 Federal energy org.
28 Paris palace
30 Ex-Yankee catcher Howard
31 Joseph Conrad's "___ of Six"
34 Dr.'s orders
35 Bard's nightfall
38 Antioxidant in foods
39 Pitcher who gave up Aaron's 715th home run
40 Roosevelt in the White House
41 "Czech Rhapsody" composer Bohuslav
44 Belle of the ball
45 Cool stretches
46 Symmetric brain parts
47 NASA city
50 Shad delicacy
52 Shop sign shorthand
53 Ones into ranch dressing?
54 Bon Jovi's "___ Life"
58 Theaters of ancient Greece
59 Prig
64 Santa ___ winds

2 "ALL YOU NEED IS . . ." by Pete Muller
The answer to 55 Across would make a good alternate title.

ACROSS

1 Film fish
6 Flambé fixer
10 Free feline?
14 Ishmael's half-brother
15 OR need
16 Some Scottish votes
17 Helena Bonham Carter movie
20 They're not needed for acoustic shows
21 Went up
22 Blue
23 Wheatback, for one
24 Shoot out
25 Famous Louvre marble
29 CEO's degree
32 Shows approval
33 It can be added to pay
34 Not mod.
35 Half in front?
36 With extreme passion
38 It might glow
39 Tea type
40 Exist
41 "Catscratch ___" (Ted Nugent album)
42 A safety gets you two
43 Baroque instrument
46 Pirate hanged in 1701
47 Irritate
48 Sue, usually, but not in a Johnny Cash song
51 Extra: Abbr.
52 Bit
55 Thompson Twins album
58 Swann who could catch a pigskin
59 Home of Interpol
60 "Definitely Maybe" is their debut album
61 Young girl
62 Last year, on Jan. 1
63 Martini's partner

DOWN

1 Feeble fellow
2 It's worth seven extra armies in "Risk"
3 Annoying ones
4 Morse bit
5 Nonplayer in the Old Globe Theater
6 Virtuous, to some
7 Build up
8 NT book
9 Boston song
10 Provide a chair for
11 Marseilles milk
12 Contact org.
13 "Gimme ___"
18 O'er in the distance
19 Cookie seen in "Rounders"
23 A famous reindeer
24 Planter place
25 At-home TV monitor
26 Put in place
27 When repeated, squeals
28 She might be super
29 "Great job!"
30 Haying machine
31 Worship
34 Leitmotif
36 Ladylike
37 MLB 2007 AL MVP
41 Be attracted to
43 Extremely yucky
44 Passionate
45 She had a hit with "White Flag"
46 Hot-dog name
48 Sate
49 "Caribbean Blue" singer
50 Olympus et al.: Abbr.
51 "Cornflake Girl" singer Tori
52 Go for a ringer
53 They hope you don't remember Alamo
54 American Indian
56 Yup
57 Thai neighbor

3 LOTS IN TRANSLATION   by Bonnie L. Gentry
12 Down has been called the "Greatest Spectacle in Racing."

ACROSS

1 Raptors, e.g.
5 It may part the waves
9 Check the mailbox for
14 Turin neighbor
15 Ending with buck or stink
16 "Games People Play" author
17 Garfield's birthday extravaganza?
20 Woman of questionable values
21 Hormuz, e.g.: Abbr.
22 Clark and Orbison
23 Multiple choice, say
26 Heckle sibilantly
28 Leave a mess on the stove?
34 Completely lose patience
35 One in Orléans
36 Band together
38 Slangy smoke
39 Vigilant
42 Vote from an anti
43 Swedish sedans
45 It merged with GE in 1986
46 Maneater of myth
47 Near a VFW post?
51 Olympic swimmer's assignment
52 Part of an archipelago
53 Plotter in a play
56 Rocky Mountains Indian
58 Muchachas: Abbr.
62 Dixieland breakfast for factory workers?
66 Ice-cold
67 1492 trio member
68 "Zip-___-doo-dah . . ."
69 Certain locks
70 Shipped off
71 Can't forgo

DOWN

1 It shows RPMs
2 Biblical barterer
3 "The Practice" roles: Abbr.
4 Slip-up
5 Potent java, slangily
6 Table scrap
7 Scale in which topaz is 8
8 Clare who married Henry Luce
9 Washboard muscles
10 Passes slowly, as a day
11 The Ponte Vecchio spans it
12 500-mile race
13 Julia's role in "Ocean's Twelve"
18 Open hearing, in law
19 "The Angry Hills" novelist
24 Use a Taser on
25 Chinese secret society
27 Carb source, informally
28 Bronze mil. medals
29 Room-sized computer
30 Katey of "8 Simple Rules . . ."
31 Transmitter starter
32 Hint of hue
33 Jump involuntarily
37 Peer group?
39 Mythical mount
40 When Mercutio delivers the Queen Mab speech
41 Team encouragement
44 Isaac Asimov's neckwear
46 Hire too many
48 Ample, in dialect
49 View from Jackson Hole
50 If follower, in computer programs
53 Rock singer ___ Pop
54 51, for one
55 Organ in tadpoles but not frogs
57 Put-in-Bay's lake
59 It gets high every day
60 Toward one side of a ship
61 Husky's load
63 Old radical org.
64 Former NASCAR airer
65 It may be hard on a construction worker

4 THE YOKE'S ON THEM   by Sam Bellotto Jr.
"Bones" is the nickname of 38 Across.

ACROSS

1 Festoon
5 Ice-cream mold
10 Pack tight
14 Stratosphere High Roller sound
15 Parliament closer
16 Piazza di Venezia locale
17 Dominant religion of Greece
20 "Walls of Jericho" group
21 Routing word
22 Suds
23 Journal offerings
26 Rumford–Bangor dir.
27 Manhattan breakfast order
32 Snake venom, e.g.
35 Teensy amount
36 First full spring mo.
37 Current law
38 Kirk's doctor friend
40 Square mileage stat
41 Uma's role in "Pulp Fiction"
42 Chinese export
43 Rock legend Holly
44 2004 World Series winners
48 A touch
49 Upgrade, in a manner of speaking
53 Emotional shocks
57 Constrictive neckwear?
58 Juan's vee
59 Goldfinger's "Goldfinger" goal
62 Homophone of I'll
63 Make up for
64 City SE of New Delhi
65 1962 NL homer leader
66 Basketry twig
67 Mattel products

DOWN

1 Asseverate
2 Atlantic City high roller
3 "The Fox and the Grapes" author
4 Tennis retrieval
5 Revealing
6 Showy
7 "Winterset" hero
8 Sharp comment
9 Heartfelt appeal
10 Gloated
11 Gander Mountain gear
12 One way to run
13 Long, for short
18 Mineral water
19 Egyptian dye
24 Stats for Derek Jeter
25 Mackintosh
28 Locks in Sault Ste. Marie
29 Fat in the can?
30 Opinion page
31 Peek inside
32 Lara Croft target
33 Kentucky neighbor
34 Yule
38 Second largest of the Philippines
39 Bathroom cleaner brand
40 One of the Horae
42 "Me too!"
43 Sacha Baron Cohen film
45 Some surgical implants
46 Prep a salmon steak
47 Warehouse worker
50 Fielding-practice bat
51 Tusk substance
52 Lubbock's state
53 Bookbinding step
54 John Jasper's pupil
55 With proficiency
56 Vince Carter et al.
60 Faith, at Lourdes
61 "Love Story" singer McPhee

PUZZLE PUN   by Ed Early

The "Golden Prosperity" tower at 4 Down is located in Shanghai.

ACROSS

1 The Boston ___
5 Disorderly in appearance
11 Nutrition abbr.
14 Exam for budding attorneys
15 Madrid locale
16 Pres. monogram of 1881
17 **Start of pun about a puzzle**
20 At a bargain price
21 Clown's leg, at times
22 May of Hollywood
23 Atlantic City mecca (with "The")
26 "I cannot tell ___"
27 **Part 2 of pun**
30 Endings for sultan
31 "I was ___ come, so here I am"
32 Parisian pronoun
33 Half the North Pole exports?
35 Fox-trot maneuver
38 Sunday talk
39 Gyro bread
40 **Part 3 of pun**
45 Hawaiian goose
46 Tolkien creature
47 Shrubs of the heath family
48 Have distaste for
50 City on San Francisco Bay
51 **End of pun**
55 Norwich loc.
56 Walking
57 Nerve network
58 "Die Another ___" (2002)
59 Legislators
60 Sugar suffixes

DOWN

1 Catcher on a table
2 Kiss
3 Has some
4 The Jin Mao Tower has 88
5 Practice a dance movement
6 "Let us leave ___ came"
7 Mailman's org.
8 Feather's partner
9 Linking word
10 Legs, to oglers
11 Montreal university
12 Rayed flower
13 Squealed
18 Capital of Yemen
19 "Give ___": Try
23 Introduce
24 "___ as You Love Me": Backstreet Boys
25 Singer Watley
28 Word root
29 PM times
33 Casino action
34 "What's Hecuba to him ___ to Hecuba": Shak.
35 Bishoprics
36 "See you then!"
37 Manège maneuvers
38 Three-time PGA champ
39 Ancestor of poker
40 "We thought they'd never ___ sing and dance . . ."
41 "Romeo and Juliet" setting
42 It may be chemical or kinetic
43 Serfs
44 ___-raspberry juice
49 Brit. medals
50 Ages and ages
52 Before PQR
53 Buffalo Bills' old org.
54 "Rock and Roll, Hoochie ___": Derringer

6 NO FOUR-LETTER WORDS   by Harvey Estes
All answers in this low-word count challenger are five letters or longer.

ACROSS

1 Some protests
6 Gathers together
11 Produce milk
13 Daily allowance
15 Belongs
16 Cold brew
17 Small bit
18 They're often smart
19 Yap
20 Red light of the night
21 Janis Ian song (with "At")
23 Take off
24 Feeling, Italian-style
25 Tasty bits
27 Possession question
29 "Buck up!"
33 Submersible tube
38 Swinton in "Michael Clayton"
39 Of a region
42 Two-base game
44 Ford part
45 Drones come out of it
46 Short operatic piece
47 Click beetles
48 Came to a boil
49 Starting points
50 Links challenge
51 Leaves in
52 Burning balls of gas

DOWN

1 Cheeky pairs?
2 Make
3 First Christian martyr
4 Large-scaled game fish
5 Bethlehem, for example
6 Sandy type
7 Self-made orphan of the Greeks
8 In all likelihood
9 Exact
10 Cassandra, e.g.
11 Speech therapy targets
12 First name in cosmetics
13 Works by Nicola or Giovanni
14 Difficult shot
22 Gush
26 Stops on the interstate
28 Party person
29 Grand ones, perhaps
30 White-tie, say
31 Stuart Little, for one
32 Most like streaking?
34 Least
35 Stone name
36 Seconds
37 Reasoner partner, once
38 "Ain't Too Proud ___": Temptations hit
40 Gorge
41 Very much
43 Ski start

7 ELECTRICAL ENGINEERING by Jim Leeds
29 Down is a good example of a misleading clue.

ACROSS

1 Give up the football
5 Rotisserie part
9 Kentucky college
14 Open up ___ of worms
15 Pas ___ (ballet step)
16 "___ Care": Tanguay
17 Shut out
19 Dogpatch rows
20 The savvy electrician ___?
22 Japanese volcano
23 Hush-hush maritime org.
24 "Aqua Teen" character
25 Gunny's rnk.
28 Electric Kathleen Winsor romance?
32 Skateboard pad
33 Uncommon, to Horace
34 Épée cousin
37 "___ drunk walks into a bar . . ."
39 Polo teams
40 Kind of dance
41 Take root
43 Electric state song of Kansas?
48 Rousing shout
49 Driver's complete turnaround
50 Nancy's friend
51 NBA center Ming
54 Con Edison's balance sheet listings?
58 They're often blue
60 Wall eyesores
61 Inspiring fear
62 What to stick it in the water
63 Filmmaker Riefenstahl
64 Hypnotized
65 Lincoln and Johnson: Abbr.
66 Detached portico

DOWN

1 Jeremy Irons movie
2 Graphic symbols
3 "Take Good ___ My Baby" (1961 hit)
4 Had the answer
5 IV solutions
6 Like the "b" in "bull" and the "p" in "parcel"
7 Ingrid's 1942 role
8 A step up from a tween
9 Centaur or mermaid, e.g.
10 Genesis locale
11 "The Social Contract" author
12 Cut short
13 Sobriety org.
18 Relating to a Greek ensemble
21 "Star Trek" producer Behr
26 Boxer's warning
27 Social receptions
29 Where Stephen King went to college
30 Jagged-edged
31 Antler part
34 Suffix for smack
35 Satirist Mort
36 It's punched at work
38 Water purification method
39 Polish off
42 Durango dishes
44 Bottle for baby
45 Thrice: Comb. form
46 Laughing predators
47 Grommet
52 "Lisa Bonet ____ basil (palindrome)
53 Easier to play, musically
55 Combined, in Calais
56 Andrea's boyfriend in "The Devil Wears Prada"
57 Coins of Peru
58 ___ d'esprit (witticism)
59 Fabric suffix

8 TALKING BIG by Ray Hamel
. . . with big words.

ACROSS

1 Went back out
6 Toothbrush maker
11 Tar
14 "Thunderball" villain
15 Not a social butterfly
16 Bride's response
17 Empty boasting
19 Bronx attraction
20 Highly regarded
21 Chain selling Martha Stewart products
23 Foal's mother
24 Heed
26 "Racer's Edge" sloganeer
29 Pretentious boasting
35 The out crowd
37 Got a perfect score on
38 Loaf end
39 Terminal man?
40 Noah in "Sergeant York"
41 "And that's all there ___ it!"
42 Dog biter
43 Bit of elementary Latin
44 Journalist's hope
45 Vain boasting
48 "The Masque of the Red Death" author
49 Some special agts.
50 Third baseman's asset
52 Runner Kip Keino's homeland
55 Like some cafe dining
60 Logical beginning?
61 False boasting
64 Pulver's rnk. in "Mister Roberts"
65 Egg-shaped
66 Baseball manager Francona
67 Ex follower
68 Landlord payments
69 Consort of Elizabeth I

DOWN

1 North Sea tributary
2 Jail window obstructions
3 Little snip
4 Incited (with "on")
5 Folded corners
6 Quaint adjective
7 Large cross
8 Mandela's polit. party
9 Waikiki welcome
10 Shattered
11 City near the Great Pyramids
12 Glade's enemy
13 Diamond flaw?
18 Target practice need
22 Kind of proportions
24 Underworld code of silence
25 Trunk
26 Up to ___ (acceptable)
27 Magnetic unit
28 Smooth one's feathers
30 Subordinate deity
31 Vast expanse
32 Slave who told tales
33 Droid's last name?
34 Skip a big wedding
36 Having open windows, maybe
40 Unadorned
44 Saw-toothed
46 Key of Beethoven's 7th
47 A little batty
51 Apportions (out)
52 More than suspected
53 One of a few "choice" parts?
54 Small victory margin
55 Buckling down
56 Slangy hats
57 Letter opener
58 Reactor section
59 Banded mineral
62 Abbr. on a Monopoly board
63 One in the cooler

9 INNER TUBES by Barry C. Silk
The theme reveals itself at 61 Down.

ACROSS

1 Tubular pasta
5 Sailor's "stop!"
10 Poet Lazarus
14 Yemen port
15 Stomach
16 Visualized
17 H.S. junior's test
18 Tabernacle locale
19 Like window dummies
20 Sweet potato, for one
23 "Affirmative"
25 Society page word
26 "No bid," in bridge
27 Cylinder-head part
32 Oboe and bassoon
33 The Buckeye State
34 White House monogram (1881–85)
37 Propagated
38 Machinist's tool
40 Shades from the sun
41 Long-distance inits.
42 Salary
43 One of the original Beach Boys
44 "The Man From U.N.C.L.E." star
47 "Peer Gynt" playwright
50 Fix illegally
51 Moe Berg's org.
52 Bay of Naples landmark
57 Taking action
58 JFK Library designer
59 Jigger of whiskey
62 Celebrate
63 Regional flora and fauna
64 ICBM type
65 MacMurray of "My Three Sons"
66 John who sang "Rocket Man"
67 PC "brains"

DOWN

1 Nuke
2 Driver's licenses, e.g.
3 Page with a perforated edge
4 Mad about
5 Reduces
6 Luxurious fabric
7 Essen elder
8 Foundry refuse
9 Item in a boot
10 Prison break, e.g.
11 Peach ___ (dessert)
12 Military messes
13 Peruvian peaks
21 Burden sometimes "on you"
22 VCR successor
23 San Francisco's ___ Buena Island
24 Bring to bear
28 Sum up
29 Primary participant
30 "Say ___"
31 Top-Flite position
34 Merchant vessel
35 Egyptian crosses
36 Orgs.
38 Research room
39 Census-form question
40 Symbol for torque
42 Refuses to
43 Trio in Bethlehem
44 Leased
45 Closely following
46 Vance of "I Love Lucy"
47 Departing words
48 Embarrassing mistake
49 Honeymoon quarters
53 Unspecific feeling
54 Jannings in "The Blue Angel"
55 Primer dog
56 Camp Lejeune letters
60 Sch. named for a televangelist
61 Tubes

10 MONEY CACHE* by Alan Olschwang
Asterisked clues relate to the title.

ACROSS

1 Medics
5 Dalmatian feature
9 Defense's focal point
14 Infante of baseball
15 Nautical greeting
16 Where Celtics deplane
17 Publish successively*
19 Scrat's "Ice Age" quest
20 Psyche
21 Ashen
22 "Ouch, that ___!"
23 Bushido practitioner
25 Office group
26 Visual arthropod organs*
31 Family cars
34 Algonquian language
35 Caduceus org.
36 Hebrew month
37 Suffix for alien
38 ___ Kross (rock group)
39 Netman Henman
40 Avian mimic
42 Superdome team
44 2005 Lisa Kudrow film*
47 Letters from Patrai
48 Loudly
52 Some brass
55 Organic compound
56 Forest denizen
57 Watchful
58 Radar's favorite drink*
60 Actress Braga
61 Italian noble name
62 Pub potions
63 Traction aid
64 Instrument of title
65 Attention getter

DOWN

1 Apothecary measures
2 Resistance symbol
3 Billiards stroke
4 ___ Lanka
5 Respectful bows
6 Writer Roth
7 Seep
8 Abilene suburb
9 Dessert option
10 Area
11 "Young Frankenstein" hunchback
12 A Maverick
13 Taverns
18 Chef's cover
22 Unit of loudness
24 The Golden Bears, shortly
25 Unadulterated
27 Two quartets
28 Tale
29 Give off
30 Fresh language
31 Bullock of "Deadwood"
32 Charles Lamb
33 Empty a certain truck
37 Miller and Martin
38 Buss
40 "It's on me!"
41 Some voters
42 Pried
43 Like shortstops
45 Illinois city
46 Genetic
49 Super stars
50 Silver streaks
51 Matzo's lack
52 Latin noun gen.
53 MP's pursuit
54 "Fascination" singer Morgan
55 Scottish Gaelic
58 Dropout's deg.
59 Easy mark

THE NAME GAME   by Doug Peterson
37 Across is also baseball's all-time leader in runs scored.

ACROSS

1 Passel
5 Tiara sparklers
9 Note above C
14 Spell checker's find
15 Declare bluntly
16 Durance of "Smallville"
17 Stench
18 Slot machine alternative
20 1979 Best New Artist Grammy winner
22 "Big" Hawaiian
23 ABA member
24 Rabbit's foot
25 Crime-fighting org.
27 Spring bloom
31 Sounds of hesitation
34 Lanai
36 Their ads often feature cavemen
37 Baseball's all-time stolen-base leader
40 Research money
41 Dismay
42 High school subj.
43 Rebuke to Brutus
44 Succor
45 Three-sided sail
47 Felix, for one
49 Glossy paint
53 Kipling's brave mongoose
58 Quit until tomorrow
59 Bearing
60 One with bad looks?
61 Have emotions
62 Klein of fashion
63 Iraqi seaport
64 Like the Sears Tower
65 Badminton barriers

DOWN

1 Fabled baby deliverer
2 Kingdom of Croesus
3 Period of time
4 Prepare
5 Made a gift of
6 Old Nick's knack
7 Current fashion
8 ___' Pea (Popeye's adoptee)
9 Warehouse
10 Unsettled region
11 Take a shine to
12 High cards
13 La Brea gunk
19 Town east of Santa Barbara
21 Sulking
25 Playing surface
26 ___ fide
28 Get out of bed
29 Clickable image
30 iPod selection
31 Egg on
32 Trumpeter Al
33 "Beat it!"
35 Hailing from Bangkok
36 Zodiacal twins
38 Tim Wakefield pitch
39 1941 Spencer Tracy role
44 Plugging away
46 Dynamic Duo member
48 "Ran" Director Kurosawa
50 Portland's state
51 The Oscars, e.g.
52 Queues
53 Hindu melody
54 Misfortunes
55 Electee of 1908
56 "What's the big ___?"
57 Film critic Pauline
58 Corn core

ACROSS

1 Reduced
5 Starfleet Academy student
10 Simba's supper
13 Biker's route
14 Nikko attraction
15 Fowl piece
16 "You Bet Your Life" host
18 Editor's conclusion?
19 Cochise's tribe
20 Word form for white stuff
21 Court fig.
22 Sea palm, for one
24 Assign
26 **Start of a quotation by 16 Across**
32 Cabinet dept.
33 Subj. for U.S. newcomers
34 Sign of late summer
35 Cpl.'s boss
36 One learning the ropes
39 Bourg is its capital
40 Be responsible for
42 Mrs. lobster
43 French ETO battleground
44 **More of quotation**
48 Male
49 Montana national forest
50 Hudson River fish
52 Steve Case's former org.
54 Field of greens
58 Finger-lickin' luau food
59 **End of quotation**
61 Further
62 Long-armed apes
63 Snakeless isle
64 Short answer
65 As like ___ (probably)
66 FedExed

DOWN

1 Lorena Ochoa's org.
2 Old West's Wyatt
3 Greek colonnade
4 Oyster-bar job
5 Comedienne Margaret
6 SALT component
7 Ross, Rigg, and Dors
8 Sign up with the registrar
9 Lone Star handle
10 They may attend galas
11 Skillfully done
12 Rough on the eyes
14 Pea-picking job
17 Emeril or Wolfgang
21 First Japanese ambassador to the U.S.
23 City on the Arno
25 Not on tape
26 "The Gondoliers" mezzo
27 Stevens in "The Farmer's Daughter"
28 Parking monitors
29 Statesman Root
30 Hardly awkward
31 Social blunders
36 Hamlet
37 Goldman on "Family Guy"
38 Lays to rest
41 Friend of Rat and Mole
43 Actress Lindsay, and kin
45 Natural aptitudes
46 Japanese inn
47 Doghouse denizen?
50 Fix a feline
51 Make perfect
53 Late-night icon
55 Beard
56 "Come ___, the water's fine!"
57 Have too little
59 World's most massive mountain
60 CAA or CIA employee

13 "PLEASE DROP IN!" by Ernest Lampert
44 Across has been called "Pavlova of the Ice."

ACROSS

1 Ike's out
6 Puccini's Floria
11 Advanced degree
14 Run to
15 Davenport occupant
16 Bill partner
17 Dabs of medium?
19 Gepetto's tool
20 Senior diplomats
21 Torpid
23 Do boring work
25 "7 Faces of Dr. ___"(1964 movie)
26 Epiphany
29 Cardinals +7, e.g.?
35 Elm extentions
37 Sq. bisector
38 Deuterium discoverer
39 You, amongst Friends
40 Wonderlands
41 Alouette, in English
42 Ponderosa guy
43 Spin-off of a sort
44 1920s–30s Winter Olympics star
45 The puck stops here?
48 Pot opener
49 Childcare writer LeShan
50 Khartoum's river
52 Hivelike
57 Astaire-Rogers musical
61 "___ Loser": Beatles hit
62 Taxis looking for a fare?
64 McGraw of baseball
65 Tomato blight
66 Musical pair
67 NYSE debut
68 Oozy
69 "Return of the Jedi" locale

DOWN

1 Minimally
2 Bats
3 "Lord knows ___!"
4 Company that coined the word "aspirin"
5 Malady
6 Idiosyncrasy
7 Cry over spilled milk
8 Babe Ruth's sultanate
9 Product books
10 Patron Saint of Scandinavia
11 Sweet Sixteen org.
12 Hamlet's cousin
13 Partner of Rinehart and Winston
18 "Peace ___ hand"
22 Little lump
24 "Rose ___": Stephen King
26 Even if, for short
27 Greeting to a spouse
28 "It's ___ Unusual Day"
30 Reunion attendee
31 Card game also called sevens
32 "Destry Rides Again" author
33 Out of this world
34 Moppets
36 Orchard measure
40 Cadillac SUV
44 Abelard's beloved
46 Brings out
47 In ___ (undisturbed)
51 Canon rival
52 NYC-based bank
53 Shoot-___ (western)
54 Como is one
55 "A flash of dew, ___ or two . . .": Dickinson
56 D. Do-Right's outfit
58 Ziegfeld's first wife
59 1968 self-titled folk album
60 Boris or Basil
63 Skate in water

14 REBUS PUZZLE by Nancy Salomon & Michael Langwald
Thematic rebus answers in the style of the game show "Concentration."

ACROSS

1 Wall St. wheeling-dealings
5 Recipe meas.
9 Cockney chap
14 Verdi opera set in Egypt
15 Overhead light?
16 Ward off
17 Neatnik's opposite
18 Not too much
19 Hot spots
20 **"Is everything okay?"**
23 Help for the irregular
24 Splits
25 Half a couple
28 Talk trash to
29 Letters of credit
31 Prufrock's creator
33 Sports figures
35 Non-pro?
36 **"Something troubling you?"**
42 Miscellaneous mixture
43 Form a union
44 Heightens
48 Needle-nosed fish
49 Stock figure
52 Enron's former NYSE symbol
53 Scandalous company
55 Clued in
57 **"Are those tears I see?"**
60 Stage
62 Spreadsheet figures
63 Take the booby prize
64 Squad car sound
65 Heroic saga
66 Whole lot
67 Plains shelter
68 Not up to snuff
69 Silver skates pursuer Brinker

DOWN

1 Scolded
2 Neil Simon play locale
3 A non-alcoholic beer
4 Native Israeli
5 Warm up
6 The Sultan of Swat
7 Water-park attraction
8 Packing a punch
9 Look through books
10 Dolly of "Hello, Dolly!"
11 Willingness to hear new ideas
12 Starr in the news
13 Some commuter trains
21 Goes off
22 Dict. entries
26 Unthinking repetition
27 Hooha
30 Feedbag morsel
32 Kenny Rogers hit
33 "That's enough!"
34 Do the math
36 Had on
37 Defender Dershowitz
38 Sc-fi plot device
39 Attractive, in a way
40 Support, of a sort
41 Lineup
45 Unflappable
46 A, in Arles
47 Goody-goodies
49 Deejay's bribe
50 Up and at 'em
51 Makes arrangements for more of "Us"
54 Relative of a giraffe
56 Cardiff residents
58 "Got it"
59 Pool tool
60 L.A. hours
61 Get a move on, quaintly

15 HAPPY FEET by Billie Truitt
"Sorry, no dancing penguins here!"

ACROSS

1 Walk laboriously
5 "Look what I did!"
9 Letter-shaped steel girder
14 Move, in realtor's lingo
15 Will beneficiary
16 ___ Carta
17 Pernicious
18 Formerly, formerly
19 One who went to market?
20 Family-size apartments
23 Licorice substitute
24 Author of the "Earth's Children" series
25 Word on a towel, perhaps
28 Actress Arthur
29 Indolent idlers
33 Grape plants
34 Greenspan or Arkin
35 Painter's tool
38 Spots at the doctor's office?
41 Mysteries in the skies
42 Talk big
43 Respond to a crisis, figuratively
47 Chemical suffix
50 "___ you all right?"
51 Follow orders
52 Desert pit stop
54 Plunger targets
58 Teach one-on-one
60 Bay bobber
61 Ingrid's "Casablanca" role
62 Click "send"
63 Old Ford models
64 Down Under greeting
65 Six a.m., for most
66 In ___ (actually)
67 Brings home

DOWN

1 Like a modular home
2 Met maestro James
3 Joan Fontaine's sister
4 Distributes
5 One of TV's Huxtables
6 Space or sol prefix
7 Causes perturbation
8 Scheming
9 Graceful antelope
10 Can of worms?
11 Off-white shade
12 Film director Lee
13 Merry month
21 Ignited once more
22 Sky lion
26 "Dies ___"
27 ID thief's targets
30 Hill dweller
31 Capital of Zimbabwe?
32 Allegro
33 One piece of a three-piece suit
35 Cougar
36 At a distance
37 San Antonio beer
38 Pop's partner
39 "The Raven" poet, initially
40 Part of PTA
42 They may be leveraged
44 Like some wages
45 Recede
46 Small, rounded stone
47 Tristan's love
48 Scratches excessively
49 English class assignments
53 Adjust precisely
55 Hard work
56 Fishing poles
57 The Big Board, briefly
58 Summer shirt
59 Thurman of "Pulp Fiction"

16 NUMERICAL ALPHABET by Pancho Harrison
A tricky theme from this Denver puzzler.

ACROSS

1 Like Heidi
6 In the center of
10 Broad-topped hill
14 Call ___ to (stop)
15 Sitar selection
16 Woes
17 Root of all evil
18 Grab (with "onto")
19 Java neighbor
20 1927 Gershwin song used in 1957's "Funny Face"
22 Natural in craps
24 Tennis great Sampras
25 Golda of Israel
26 Some insurance frauds
29 Kind of jump shot
33 Last words of "The Purple Cow"
34 1962 Ray Charles country hit
35 Canine comment
36 Neighbor of Turkey
37 AOL alternative
38 1930 Gershwin song from "Girl Crazy"
41 Levi Dockers feature, often
43 Parsley family herb
44 Erin Moran TV role
45 Cotton bundle
46 Residential area, for short
47 "Ta-ta"
50 1971 Carole King song from "Tapestry"
54 Rice-A-___
55 Fork feature
57 Love poetry muse
58 Freudian topics
59 "Animal House" party attire
60 Jacket worn by Sammy Davis Jr.
61 Laundry load
62 City near Provo
63 Have confidence in

DOWN

1 ___ Club (Costco rival)
2 "How'd the game end?"
3 ". . . ___ my Annabel Lee": Poe
4 Consider overnight
5 Synthetic rubber component
6 Debate
7 Teen hangout
8 "May ___ now?"
9 Barry Humphries alter ego
10 Left-winger
11 Norway's patron saint
12 Marseilles miss: Abbr.
13 Speller's clarifying phrase
21 Knox and Dix: Abbr.
23 Not be truthful with
25 One of the Osmonds
26 Addis ___, Ethiopia
27 Summer TV fare
28 The first or fifth letter of George, e.g.
29 Pro ___ (perfunctorily)
30 Voters since 1920
31 Very, in music
32 "Fiddler on the Roof" matchmaker
34 One way to take an enemy outpost
36 Short dagger
39 Woody Allen stereotype
40 Oil of ___
41 Omen
42 Working stiff
44 Roast beef au ___
46 Second stringers
47 Cold one
48 Exercise discipline with asanas
49 Slaughter of baseball
50 "Picnic" playwright
51 Pearl Harbor's site
52 Alphabet components: Abbr.
53 Went to Wendy's, say
56 Suffix with super

17 OUT OF THIS WORLD   by Alan Olschwang
18 Down is often depicted holding an ankh.

ACROSS

1 Gave a flip
6 Gym dance
9 Guy
14 Primitive calculators
15 "Xanadu" band
16 Actor Delon
17 Delicate fern
19 1969 role for Dustin
20 Peyton Manning's brother
21 Corrida competitor
22 Enclosed by
23 Some Louvre hangings
25 Charged particle
26 Governments of the wealthy
32 Kushner's "___ in America"
35 Ruby or Sandra
36 Fit for the task
37 Ways to get out
38 Tie the knot
39 Absinthe flavoring
40 Kind of rug
41 Crony
42 Slurs over
43 Post-WW2 economic aid program
46 Try truffles
47 Driver's need
51 Cannon of a sort
55 Expression of feigned amusement
56 "The Black Cat" auth.
57 Eschew
58 Melancholy
60 Slow in music
61 "Roses ___ red . . ."
62 Oncle's wife
63 Prepare for a match
64 Some enlistees
65 Assuages

DOWN

1 Speleologist
2 White poplar
3 Collared
4 Old French coin
5 Makes gin
6 San Simeon builder
7 Olla podrida
8 ___ favor
9 Cooked cereal
10 Israeli seaport
11 Thin wood strip
12 Virna in "Arabella"
13 Soon
18 Falcon-headed Egyptian god
22 Had on
24 Massenet works
25 On the rocks
27 Digger of old-time radio
28 Eyetooth
29 Footnote abbr.
30 Otherwise
31 Understands
32 First grandfather
33 "Key Largo" heroine
34 Attendee
38 "Van Wilder" director Becker
39 Dining option
41 Early forerunner of Leno
42 Root from New York
44 Confrontational
45 Franklin Mint products
48 Hamburg refusals
49 End of a French toast
50 Wired blades
51 Scotch, for one
52 Concluded
53 Anagram name of 33 Down
54 Tail-twining monkey
55 Last name in spydom
58 Reagan's first presidency
59 Pilots' org.

18 DENNIS RODMAN'S 2004 WIN   by Brad Wilber
. . . and he received $222,000 for that win at 17 Down.

ACROSS

1 1969 Joyce Carol Oates novel
5 Sucker punch, e.g.
14 ___ avis
15 Violin bow material
16 Saint canonized in 993
18 Mitochondrion or vacuole, e.g.
19 Heavenly altar
20 Novel which inspired "Clueless"
22 San Francisco mayor Newsom
23 Like bath mats
25 Put through the blender
26 Rip to pieces
27 Wellsian fruit eaters
29 Under an alcohol ban
30 Second-string player
31 Cloud of negativity?
33 Green car
37 Cricket batsman position
38 Covers with black grime
40 Alarm settings, for short
43 Meadow Soprano's dad
44 Attire
45 Coolers
47 Hot air
48 Father of Hector
49 Mythical goat-man
50 Kennel exclamation
51 Saran Wrap targets
54 Took a chance
56 Rakes with gunfire
57 "Ta-ta!"
58 Grand-piano pedal
59 Ian in "Lord of the Rings"

DOWN

1 Certain cutters
2 "Our Gang" producer
3 Quixote's specialty
4 Month during le printemps
5 Emulate Pac-Man
6 Bar mitzvah dance
7 0.1 microjoule
8 Simile center
9 Anatole France satire
10 Wool-gather?
11 Split 50-50
12 More sycophantic
13 In
17 Dennis Rodman's 2004 win
21 Successor to Salyut 7
24 Multiplex mementos
25 Milne protagonist
27 Diplomatic agent
28 Creditor's claim
31 Mideast's Gulf of ___
32 Hotfoot it
34 Altar exchange
35 Casanova
36 Like Glinda the Good Witch
39 Bottom rung, in the Middle Ages
40 Waldorf salad ingredients
41 Rita in "Carnal Knowledge"
42 Solo racing boats
44 Actor Gulager
46 "Weird Al" Jackson song parody
47 Sarastro in "The Magic Flute," e.g.
49 Wring one's hands
52 Grace ___ Owen ("L.A. Law" role)
53 End of many e-mail addresses
55 Oh, in Cologne

19 THREE MEN IN A TUB   by Jim Leeds
And who do you think they be?

ACROSS

1 E-mail from Hormel?
5 Mountain spike
10 Swing
14 Pakistani language
15 Florist's draw
16 Arrow poison
17 Lampblack
18 Macanudo product
19 Thom the loafer?
20 The butcher admits ___
23 Pray
24 Japanese-American
25 "Arms and the Man" playwright
26 "Gladiator" director
30 Veggie served with 1 Down
31 Kind of wagon
33 Roy Orbison hit
34 Livingston in "Office Space"
35 The baker is ___
39 Early sixth-century date
40 Muslim republic
41 Kyushu volcano
42 Word in Montana's motto
43 Precincts
45 "Ibis" poet
48 Good for something
50 PETA prefers them faux
53 The candlestick maker ___
57 ". . . ___ may never meet again" (Johnny Mathis lyric)
58 A wolf raised him
59 Former "Wheel of Fortune" host
60 Reach a maximum
61 CORE leader Roy
62 Savvy about
63 Former Russ. states
64 Michael in "The Quiet American"
65 Deprivation

DOWN

1 Raw fish dish
2 Prefaces
3 Brewer Coors
4 Mangle
5 Certain horse in a race
6 Van Gogh masterpiece
7 Roman coverup
8 It abuts Yemen
9 Fragrant ointment
10 Big wheels for big wheels
11 Chin cleft
12 Got tough with
13 Stress
21 Adds diacritical marks to Hebrew letters
22 Svelte
27 Carbon copy
28 "___ the fields we go . . ."
29 "Bye!"
32 Big do
35 American rates
36 Custer's Last Stand conflict
37 Raw sienna
38 Leaving
39 Comical Canadian singing duo
44 Spangle
46 Cantillate
47 PC key
49 Pursues
51 Ballet ___ de Monte Carlo
52 Bishopric group
54 Mabius of "Ugly Betty"
55 Siberian river
56 Prefix for bus

20 AN INCONVENIENT TRUTH by Larry Shearer
Be sure and watch Al Gore's documentary before solving this one.

ACROSS

1 Inexplicit
6 Shut tight
10 Fall birthstone
14 Mistreat
15 Declaration in court
16 Disaster relief org.
17 Congressional investigation?
19 Skedaddled
20 ___ empty stomach
21 Free
22 Arousing
23 Jamaican music
25 Unnatural
27 On the other hand
29 Five Nations tribe
33 Publicist's anathema
38 Dodge truck
39 Peter in "The Maltese Falcon"
40 Fool
42 Demolish
43 It merged with Chevron in 2005
45 Many St. Augustine residents
47 Rests
49 Carried the day
50 It's worth one point in Scrabble
52 Skewer morsels
57 Veteran sailor
60 De Gaulle's birthplace
62 Composer Stravinsky
63 AAA mem.
64 What a sentry might say?
66 Okefenokee possum
67 Singer Young
68 Contest spot
69 Vodka brand
70 "This ___ sudden!"
71 Fools

DOWN

1 It's in the air
2 Have ___ to pick
3 Solzhenitsyn's prison
4 Taking advantage of
5 Donne's dusk
6 Whirled
7 Crack
8 Mountaintop abodes
9 Like wedding cakes
10 One desperate for a bug spray?
11 Soccer legend
12 VISA alternative, briefly
13 ___ Day (Billie Holiday nickname)
18 Sight often seen at a theatre
24 Side by side
26 Straight
28 Disapproving sound
30 Shoreline shelter
31 Fit to ___
32 Maglie and Mineo
33 Make obscure
34 Crack
35 Discontinue
36 Hype restraint?
37 Polite address
41 Lawn coating
44 "Sweet ___" ("Wakiki Wedding" song)
46 Keepsake
48 Playground features
51 "Love Me Tender" singer
53 Coffin holders
54 Very destructive 1972 hurricane
55 Wilderness Road trailblazer
56 Sp. misses
57 Fools
58 Running ___
59 Building block
61 Composer Schifrin
65 21st President's monogram

21 JOBS OF SILICON VALLEY by Matt Ginsberg
Techies should be familiar with 40 Across.

ACROSS

1 Pocket food
5 Basque stream
9 French sight-seer
13 One seeing a lot of red
14 Calligrapher's fine points
15 Chris craft
16 Librarian's credo
19 "Annie" couple
20 Crew's control
21 Yakov Smirnoff's birthplace
22 Poly-sci finals
23 Child guidance
24 Poor judgment
27 Talked over and over
31 Like an unwatched pot
32 End notes
33 Motor attachment
34 Attractive ironwork
38 British byes
39 Four front
40 Jobs of Silicon Valley
41 Regular guys
44 Selling points
45 Fiction material
46 Advanced degrees
47 Birthday gift
50 "Cheers" stoolie
51 Beginning of a hickey
54 Householder
57 Zodiac sign
58 Razor handle
59 Broadway opening
60 Left at sea
61 Make a stink
62 Crowd noise

9 Crude ships
10 Do these justify the means
11 Urban ends
12 Turner in "Peyton Place"
15 Speaking points
17 Register ring
18 Robin's home
22 Colored part of a ball
23 Pesach feast
24 Thai cabbage
25 One trying to avoid charges
26 Code maker with a dotty history
27 Digs like pigs
28 One working on the cutting edge
29 École attendee
30 Saturday night specials
32 What the little birdie told Scrooge
35 Circus boosters
36 Intake problem
37 Mustang racers, once
42 Son of Kong
43 Buggy places
44 Barely move
46 Dame intro
47 Driving hazard
48 Dynamic beginning
49 Locale for a den mother
50 Parker in "The Great Debaters"
51 Art follower
52 Logical introduction
53 Mayberry drunk
55 Camel hazard
56 Talker's gift

DOWN

1 Example of model behavior
2 High-handed remark
3 Rolodex nos.
4 Art, nowadays
5 Put down stakes
6 Last stands
7 Mel Ott's 1,860
8 Watch this

ACROSS

1 Adjective for cell or pile
8 "I Love ___"
15 Emphatic denial
16 Article lower in a hierarchy
17 **Start of a quip by Groucho**
19 "Just a ___ at . . ."
20 Prepare the sails for another cruise
21 Train line for Nassau County, NY
22 Remains on the lee side
25 Computer keyboard key
28 **Part 2 of quip**
29 Screw thread cutter
32 Hutton in "American Gigolo"
34 Mark Twain's burial place
36 Engine at a red light
37 "None ___ the lonely heart . . ."
40 Legal scholar Guinier and others
41 Brother of Groucho
42 Chicago–Detroit dir.
43 In need of ___ of paint
44 **Part 3 of quip**
47 List ender
50 Brewery supply
51 Shin preceder
55 **End of quip**
58 Mother in "Ah, Wilderness!"
59 Crag
60 Subway rider's convenience
61 Pass a rope through a hole
62 Eon segment
63 Annoy
64 Private talk duo?
65 Deli choice
66 65 Across, for one

DOWN

1 Burgundy and Bordeaux
2 Melville novel
3 Ames or Errol
4 Sharp flavors
5 Germ or prof finish
6 Fix in the mind
7 Australian cries
8 Birthplace of St. Francis
9 Darts, for one
10 Fortas or Burrows
11 Springfield or Enfield
12 French possessive
13 Writer Earl ___ Biggers
14 Retired, as a prof.
18 Before, before
23 Oscar winner Charlize
24 Egyptian laborer
25 Shake-speare's Age: Abbr.
26 "Your Love Is King" singer
27 Cosby's "I Spy" costar
29 Martinez of baseball
30 Operatic solo
31 Tense input?
33 Loathsome
35 Solvent which decomposes food
37 Bird that likes wasps
38 Distasteful
39 Mosaic chips
45 Caustic stuff
46 Linotype feeders: Abbr.
47 "Movie Home Companion" author
48 "We're off ___ the wizard . . ."
49 No liability
52 Dropped the ball
53 Dred Scott, for one
54 Highly agitated
56 Trevino and Strasberg
57 Nickname of Hockey's Phil

23 THREE SHORT STACKS   by Bonnie L. Gentry
Breakfast just isn't the same anymore.

ACROSS

1 Bone breakers
16 Choice in academia
17 Cause trouble
18 Social or septic starter
19 CPR deliverers
20 Spawning fish
21 Alternatives to PCs
25 Mark with a branding iron
27 Immature newt
30 "The Purple People Eater" singer Wooley
32 They'll never get off the ground
36 Hard to wrinkle
41 Isn't pleasant to remember
42 Order sought by an accused before trial
43 Handyman's gadget
44 Author of "I Kid You Not"
45 Land in l'eau
46 "She's a Lady" songwriter
50 Many moons
52 Badly
55 Burned, to a nerd
57 Russian leader until 1917
61 Covered-dish supper favorite
66 Radar jamming and decoy flares, e.g.
67 When procrastinators get going

13 Short iron, for Tiger
14 Action-denoting suffix
15 Cartoonist Silverstein
22 Nincom-poops
23 Capablanca's game
24 Asian inn for caravans
26 Adjust a document setting
27 Striking success
28 Middle Corleone brother
29 "I love you," to Luis
31 Fast-tempoed jazz
33 Pastoral people of Kenya
34 Up to the point that
35 Memorial marker
37 Province of central Spain
38 Yemeni city
39 Conventioneer's badge
40 Outlet, e.g.
47 Nick of "North Dallas Forty"
48 Show obeisance
49 Capital of Ghana
51 Act the troubadour
52 Manco Capac's people
53 Pilfered goods
54 Ill-mannered oaf
56 Current blockers
58 Tender
59 Architect William Van ___
60 Conclude one's case
62 Gov. J. Shaheen's political ID
63 Shooting location
64 Houston of the Republic of Texas
65 Placido's "that"

DOWN

1 Gp. advocating adoption
2 Go to the dark side
3 "My eye!"
4 Staked thing
5 Young fox
6 Just past five o'clock?
7 "Now I've got it!"
8 What the last piggy got
9 Solicits, with "up"
10 Deliberately annoy
11 "The Gondoliers" flower girl
12 Man-mouse link

24 GIRL IN A BLUE HOUSE   by Bernice Gordon
The "Blue House" is where 17 Across lived and is now a museum.

ACROSS
1 Slipped a Mickey
6 Russell ___ College
10 Pair of mules
14 Nobelist Joliot-Curie
15 Pitchfork-shaped letters
16 Sharpen a scythe
17 "Roots" painter
19 Ponte Vecchio's river
20 Pie fruit
21 Clan wear
23 URL
27 Inhibit
28 Blubberheads?
29 Whirlybird
30 Intent
33 Oscar-winning brothers
34 Adage
35 Daughter of Cadmus
36 Frozen-waffle brand
37 Dialectics
38 Sphere start
39 The Indigo Girls, e.g.
40 Rajah's consort
41 Like the fishing cat
42 Suffix for rocket
43 Sugar bowl team?
44 "Valse ___": Sibelius
45 Ammonia compound
47 "Confounded!"
48 Witchy groups
50 "I don't give ___!"
51 Aid in a felony
52 Dolores Olmedo Patiño Museum display
58 Rail
59 "The Night of the Hunter" screenwriter
60 City on the Songka river
61 Effect a cure
62 Department in N France
63 "Ode to a Baby" poet Nash

DOWN
1 "What's the ___?"
2 Eight-time Norris Trophy winner
3 Indiana U. Museum designer
4 Terminal
5 Circus Circus employees
6 E-mails junk
7 Former Davis Cup coach
8 Indy 500 winner de Ferran
9 Recondite
10 Split up
11 17 Across was a "self" one
12 Soprano Moffo
13 Bright light
18 Rodin sculpture (with "The")
22 Smidgen
23 Give in
24 Re-entry parachute
25 Husband of 17 Across
26 Casino city
27 Land of Cotton
29 Security deposits
31 Pokey person
32 Acted cheeky?
34 ___ Carlo
37 Lubber
38 "___ stands now . . ."
40 Somerset Maugham story
41 Plains Indian
44 Gillette's ___ II razor
46 Noted conductor
47 Sun-___ tomatoes
48 Mazuma
49 "Bolero" instrument
50 Feller
53 Teamwork deterrent
54 Quarter horse not worth a nickel
55 Connective word
56 Sevruga delicacy
57 Its symbol is Sn

25 SOUPS DU JOUR   by Alan Olschwang
Chowderheads have a definite solving edge here.

ACROSS

1 Dog star
5 Nemeses
10 Commandment word
14 Gaudy
15 Make ends meet
16 Troubles
17 Where to find a good Irish stew in the Buckeye State?
19 Wait at the light
20 Actor Delon
21 Signal after the danger has passed
23 Flowers' places
26 Bread cover
27 Sticker stat
30 Where to find a good minestrone in the Peach State?
35 Vacuum's lack
36 Stadium section
37 Suit material
38 Speaker's platform
40 Social sufferers
43 Famed surrealist
44 Nullify
46 QED part
48 Low sound?
49 Where to find a good borscht in the Gem State?
52 Old French coin
53 Attired
54 Spill the beans
56 Came into view
60 Debonair
64 Lemming cousin
65 Where to find a good bouillabaisse in the Lone Star State?
68 Mild expletive
69 Musical study
70 Headland
71 They're opposed
72 Balance-sheet item
73 Safer

DOWN

1 Captain Pierce portrayer
2 Kind of music
3 Sousaphone
4 Off-the-cuff remark
5 Prohibit
6 Bother
7 Okinawa port
8 Novel ending
9 1966 U.S. Open winner
10 Personalized
11 Trapper's quest
12 Stew pot
13 Patron
18 Languid
22 Bus. leaders
24 Exhaust
25 Hook's mate
27 Palindromic address
28 Keyboard instrument
29 Beams
31 Transgressed
32 Fats units
33 Abode for Ice Cube?
34 Kindergarten quintet
39 Makes it
41 Dull
42 Funnyman Mort
45 Mr. Applegate's accomplice
47 Skoal or prosit
50 Bent out of shape
51 Conceive
55 Park of California
56 With: French
57 Cartoon possum
58 Think out
59 Clobber
61 Skater's jump
62 Roses' place
63 Latin infinitive
66 Amin of Uganda
67 Ready to run

Asterisked clues are all members of the clan.

ACROSS

1 Philosopher David (1711–1776)*
5 Noble Italian family
9 Arafat's successor
14 "Law & Order: SVU" star
15 Tiptop
16 "The Sound of Music" family
17 Disraeli's rival*
19 Certain Web surfer
20 One-horse carriages
21 "Goldfinger" star*
23 Bose rival
25 Get under one's skin
26 "Sweet Afton" poet*
30 "What's going ___ there?"
32 ___-El (Superman)
35 Langston Hughes poem
36 "A Study in Scarlet" author*
39 Lacking legal force
40 According to schedule
41 Negri in "Madame Bovary"
42 THEME
44 Prep for Kings College
45 Switch positions
46 In ___ (shortly)
47 "Rob Roy" author*
48 Maui music maker
49 Monterrey munchie
52 Subject of a Shakespeare tragedy*
56 Bay of Whales locale
61 Crazy Spanish numbers?
62 Two-time UK prime minister (1886–1937)*
64 Pay for lunch
65 Workplace protection org.
66 Shortest bk. in the Bible
67 Instructional book genre
68 "The ___ the limit!"
69 Audiometer inventor*

DOWN

1 Like falsetto
2 The Bruins' school
3 Tight-fisted
4 JFK stats
5 Cake message for Alice
6 Brindisi bride
7 X
8 Major suit?
9 Kaput
10 Yankee Stadium location
11 Christian in "Batman Begins"
12 Takeoff artist
13 Sprightly
18 Pub crawlers
22 Shropshire and Wiltshire
24 Make up
26 Parlor pastime
27 Complete reversal
28 Players play them
29 Big Easy acronym
31 Astro ending
32 Former capital of Japan
33 Shell out
34 Listed
36 Mollycoddle
37 Whenever
38 Crude group
43 Likes right off
47 Comme ci, comme ça
48 Wolfgang Lüth's vessel
50 Literary cockroach
51 Score endings
52 One not afraid of the limelight?
53 Kind of phobia
54 Masticate
55 Membership care gps.
57 High muck-a-muck
58 "¿Quien ___?" ("Who knows?")
59 Carrier to Ben-Gurion
60 Over and above: Abbr.
63 Grill

27 MIXED NUTS by Kevin George
Four theme entries relate to the title.

ACROSS

1 Stripe
6 Balkan native
10 It's a long story
14 In town
15 Banned orchard spray
16 Shrinking Asian sea
17 Bowl
18 Homer Simpson's mom
19 Rock's Jethro ___
20 Trendy
21 Action-movie stand-in
24 Gallic girlfriend
25 "Wheel of Fortune" category
26 Some like to rub it in
31 "See ya" in Sonora
32 Shakespearean verb
33 Snatch
36 Drift
37 New Orleans footballer
39 Pet plant
40 Helpful connections
41 Hwys.
42 October stones
43 "Marie Antoinette" star
46 Theater opening
49 Rogers and Clark
50 Biennial statistics
53 Poor service?
56 Inflamed ending
57 Color quality
58 Vice President before Gerald
60 Diving position
61 Whitney and Manning
62 Miniscule
63 Late Orly birds
64 "Round and Round" rock group
65 "Holy cow!"

DOWN

1 Bridge contract
2 Mower maker
3 Passed with flying colors
4 See 22 Down
5 Television varieties
6 Jackson of "Pulp Fiction"
7 North Carolina university
8 Tirade
9 "Troy" star
10 General Motors division
11 Caribbean island
12 Exasperates
13 Formal avenue
22 "Wizard of Oz" character (with 4-D)
23 "We're in trouble!"
24 Basic unit
26 It's a wrap
27 Japanese noodle
28 Vardalos and Peeples
29 Lyric poet
30 Stone weight
33 Poker expert Johnny
34 Art supplies
35 Former
37 Less forgiving
38 He lost twice to DDE
39 PC "brains"
41 Cambodian cash
42 Spacecraft orbiting Mars
43 Gifts
44 Jim Varney character
45 Commandment word
46 Jimmy of "NYPD Blue"
47 Whale constellation
48 It's handed down
51 "Return of the Jedi" dancing girl
52 Troop group
53 String together
54 Highlands dialect
55 Woody and Buzz Lightyear
59 Mile High Center architect

28 BEAT THE CLOCK 9:22 by Ernest Lampert
Consider yourself a whiz if you can solve this one in 9:22 or better.

ACROSS

1 Meat tenderizer
7 Most blue
15 Relationship involving love and jealousy
17 Retreating army's defensive maneuver
18 Prudential rival
19 Moved carefully
20 "The Pittsburgh Kid" of the ring
23 "Breakfast in Bed" artist
26 Sgt.'s address
27 Windy City team
28 Nicholas II was the last one
32 Ecological community
34 Note
36 Tchaikovsky's "___ Cantabile"
39 Tiger Woods' real first name
40 Skimmers
42 Cottonwood relative
43 Gray ___
44 Antiaircraft fire
47 Shogun's capital
48 Scale model
50 Cy Young winner Saberhagen
51 ___ the hole
54 Myanmar, in the past
56 Walks down Madison Ave.?
62 Simultaneously
63 Craving ones
64 Cinch

DOWN

1 Pricing word
2 Took the cake, say
3 Shell-game item
4 Firth of Clyde island
5 "Splendor in the Grass" screenwriter
6 Sinuous dance of the East
7 Bonn boulevard

8 Suffix for cow or can
9 ___ Fail (Irish coronation stone)
10 Be silent, in music
11 Shredded
12 Support
13 Wild plum
14 Keep an eye on
16 Maui neighbor
20 Secret doctrine
21 He speaks his mind
22 Pest
24 To a degree
25 Botanist's angle
27 Recent: Comb. form
29 SWAT team member
30 Submit
31 Make a better hitch
33 Hindu religious sage
35 Site of Theo. Roosevelt National Park
37 Drainpipe part
38 It's inside: Abbr.
41 Slopes habitués
45 Less than right?
46 Piranha
49 Key word
50 Bêtes noires
51 Mordant
52 Feature of Beldar from Remulak
53 Tolkien tree creatures
55 "September ___": Diamond
57 Honshu bay
58 Bluejacket
59 Track-and-field org.
60 Paper size: Abbr.
61 Harry Connick, Jr. album

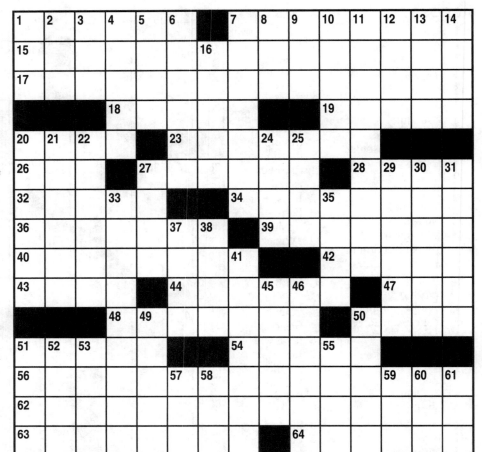

29 CAUSTIC CRITIQUE   by Ed Early
The author of the searing review below can be found at 37 Down.

ACROSS

1 Radio type
5 Irritate
10 ___ Raton
14 Stage direction
15 "The Philosophy of Right" author
16 Coup d'___
17 Trick ending
18 Persian Gulf export
20 **Start of a sardonic literary review**
22 Sp. equivalent of Frau
23 Arrive at a judgment
24 Vestiges
26 Neighborhoods
27 U.S. Public Health agcy.
30 "___ of those who . . ."
31 Orientation instruments
33 **Part 2 of review**
36 Whirling Sicilian dance
38 Gramophone inventor Berliner
39 "Treasure Island" monogram
40 Acela, for one
45 Basketball pros
47 **See 37 Down**
48 Aiport near Disney World
49 **End of review**
53 Constant busy signal, e.g.
55 Parting words
56 Guitar chord
57 Century 21 listings
58 Peter Fonda title role
59 Collision souvenir
60 ___ al-Arab (Iraqi river)
61 Foxx of Comedy

DOWN

1 Prosecutor's aide: Abbr.
2 Nurture
3 Swindle
4 Oldest of the Brady girls
5 Garlic relative
6 This spot
7 Lab gel
8 Bogs
9 Ex-governor Spitzer
10 Turpin of slapstick
11 ENT instrument
12 Egyptian capitalist?
13 Encyclopedia sections
19 Namaqualand locale
21 Binges, briefly
25 Eros
27 Prefix for space
28 Amusing, in an odd way
29 Lets the A/C run
31 Clock std.
32 Music to shuffle by
33 Shakedown cruise, for one
34 Hearty partner
35 Xenon, argon, et al.
36 Made for a mortise
37 **Author of review (with 47-A)**
40 Padre's sister
41 Serve more coffee
42 Fit for cultivation
43 1954 Patti Page hit
44 Took home
46 Certain undergrads
47 Brittany seaport
50 Cry of delight
51 Home-loan agcy.
52 "___ of wit well play'd": Shak.
54 1/3 a wine

STEWART'S GRAND CRU?   by Matt Ginsberg
The answer to that question can be found at 38 Across.

ACROSS

1 Baby swallows
5 Fake handle
10 Herb for the judicious
14 Code beginning
15 Car opener
16 City on the Oka River
17 Song tribute to Marilyn Monroe
20 Bud holder
21 "None missing"
22 Little suckers
25 Strong light
26 A many-splendored thing in Italy
30 Rice concoction
33 Brown bread
34 Buck back
35 Grande opening
38 Stewart's grand cru?
42 Switch "ups"
43 Ruler with a line
44 Head lights
45 Gas range
47 Gets across
48 Make a hash of
51 Cause of a class struggle
53 Disbelief
56 Battery components
60 Hard up
64 Spotted
65 Tax extension
66 Commedia dell'___
67 Azurite and tinstone
68 "Picnic" beauty queen
69 Stage mom in "Gypsy"

DOWN

1 Doctor's bag?
2 Brief investments
3 House opening?
4 Marquis name
5 House of games
6 A blooming necklace
7 Board seller
8 "A Bug's Life" princess
9 Satirist Mort
10 Careless catchphrase
11 First sign
12 Art class
13 Hostel opening
18 Exists from a long time ago
19 Cinder ending
23 First-rate
24 Factotum
26 Air head
27 Climactic sound
28 Crew's control
29 They stand before U
31 Evening out
32 Brick measure
35 Avis adjective
36 Coward's confession
37 Epinicia
39 J. D. holder
40 A time to dye
41 Western agreement
45 Where the buoys are
46 A bettor item
48 "Attila" operatic title role
49 Wolverine's kin
50 A one and a two
52 Plum pit
54 E-mail attack
55 Intro to physics
57 VA neighbor
58 Tropical tuber
59 They flew for nearly 35 years
61 "The butler ___ it!"
62 Bank contents
63 Half a snicker

ISLAND FEATURE   by Pete Muller
A tropical topic from this native New Yorker.

ACROSS

1 Half a dolphinfish
5 From the barrel, to Capp
10 Bridge
14 Regents, for example
15 Ukelele has one
16 Big Brown hair
17 **A collection of letters**
20 Island near Maui
21 Type of wonder
22 Some layers
25 Brass, for example
26 A Kennedy
30 Pliocene and Pleistocene
33 German beer saint
34 Pop
35 Japanese sash
38 **What's special about the collection: Part 1**
42 English Beat genre
43 Informative android?
44 Waste producer
45 One keeping track
47 Wahine's welcome
48 Where two become one
51 Pair
53 Ahi steak, e.g.
56 First name in strikeouts
60 **What's special about the collection: Part 2**
64 Last name in couture
65 Foreigner
66 They're seen at SFO
67 It's in Paris but not in New York?
68 Spay
69 When doubled, quickly

DOWN

1 Joe Cocker's "Cry ___ River"
2 It could be a double
3 LOL
4 Committing words
5 North of Virginia
6 Marcel, say
7 Spike TV, formerly
8 Staring
9 Type of platter
10 Some blouses
11 Inquiring group
12 "___ it goes . . ."
13 Informative
18 "The Prophet" poet Gibran
19 Solitude can be found here
23 Olympian drink
24 Saw
26 "Beowulf," for one
27 Go down
28 Certain skirt
29 Bridge whiz Culbertson
31 Chicago Fire scapegoat
32 Tesla namesake
35 ___ buco
36 Matt Helm's wife
37 It could be bad or good
39 Tokyo, once
40 It's shortest at noon
41 "Rhapsody in Blue" carrier: Abbr.
45 "Surfin' ___": Beach Boys
46 "Strong Enough" singer Sheryl
48 "Like me"
49 Marx brother?
50 Porsche SUV
52 Attach
54 Turtle Bay locale
55 Fossey or Parkinson
57 MGM studios cofounder
58 Intro painting class
59 Mont. neighbor
61 Perfect marks
62 Newcastle or Sierra Nevada
63 Fed. stipend

32 EMINEM by Barry C. Silk
37 Across was a 2008 Microsoft acquisition target.

ACROSS

1 Highland hats
5 Measured (with "up")
10 Karaoke need
14 Month in Israel
15 "We hold ___ truths . . ."
16 Voiced
17 Chatterbox
19 Made the putt
20 Historic beginning?
21 Butterfinger's comment
22 Ready for
24 Hungry person's query
26 MD's diagnostic tools
27 French friend
28 "P" or "D" on a coin, e.g.
32 Sine language?
35 "CSI" interruption
37 Google competitor
38 Mata ___
39 Piquant
41 Page (through)
42 DVD player button
44 Egyptian queen, for short
45 Dodge model until 1990
46 Jim Cramer show
48 Tonic's partner
50 Summer quaffs
51 Targeted
55 Mortgage payment add-on
58 Island of Napoleon's exile
59 Suffix with social
60 Alcove
61 Hollywood heavyweight
64 Surfer's sobriquet
65 Sports complex
66 Very knowledgeable
67 Practice boxing
68 Frisco footballer
69 Sam and Dave's label

DOWN

1 Devil Rays' home
2 Gussy up
3 Pirate's pal
4 Full-house letters
5 Swiss winter resort
6 Optimist's phrase
7 Supreme Greek deity
8 NYC hrs.
9 Remove a rack
10 NBA 1978–79 MVP
11 "If ___ the Zoo": Dr. Seuss
12 German philosopher
13 Nevada county
18 Space
23 Feel sorry for
25 Writing utensil for Copperfield?
26 Gnatlike insect
28 Virile
29 "Uh, excuse me?"
30 Horse of a different color?
31 UN leader Annan
32 Van Morrison's former group
33 Indian prince
34 Outraged
36 Bad habits
40 Jellystone Park denizen
43 Heading on a list of errands
47 "Seinfeld" character
49 Muslim leader
51 Dress style
52 Finger or toe
53 Pasadena neighbor
54 Fax precursor
55 Terminates
56 Mulligatawny, for one
57 Musical wrap-up
58 Roulette bet
62 ". . . ___ quit!"
63 Cries of pain

33 CHIVALRY LIVES   by Sarah Keller
The real title can be found at 54 Across.

ACROSS

1 Break fasts
4 Pinnacle
8 Movie trailer
14 Tell falsehoods
15 Well-heeled?
16 To a great degree
17 Like emergency lights
19 "It was my best effort"
20 Loose coins
22 Moving about
25 Ho's instrument
26 Neighbor of Isr.
27 Monitor option
31 Pres. Jefferson
32 Med. report
33 "___ Ben Jonson!": Young
38 Charge card term
42 Native of Yemen's capital
43 Big Band follower?
44 Clinton cabinet member Federico
45 Attendee at a pre-nuptial party
49 "Stupid me!"
52 Craggy height
53 Edward James in "Selena"
54 Chivalrous act/PUZZLE TITLE
59 Valentine message
60 Educational milieu
64 Fetches
65 "Comin' ___ the Rye"
66 Swiss peak
67 Most reasonable
68 Pt. of AAA
69 Encouragement at the bullring

DOWN

1 Pole worker
2 Feel sick
3 Surrey spot?
4 On land
5 A la mode
6 Jazzman Thelonious
7 It may be cutting
8 Alan of "Growing Pains"
9 Choice offering
10 Taj Mahal site
11 Kick targets
12 Mournful song
13 Winona in "Mr. Deeds"
18 Imitates a peeping Tom
21 S–W filler
22 Ad ___ per aspera
23 Bus station handout, for short
24 Hidden treasure
28 Reno's st.
29 Enjoy the slopes
30 Vice President Spiro
34 Turn off
35 Revoke, to a lawyer
36 Classic laundry detergent
37 Les ___-Unis
39 "TV Guide" entries
40 Test for collegiate srs.
41 Saturn or Mercury
46 "No kidding"
47 Web site address ending
48 NASCAR racer Jeff
49 "Catch-22" lieutenant
50 Horse or soap follower
51 Confine
55 Three times three
56 Computer input
57 "Talking Vietnam" singer
58 Rows
61 Long March leader
62 Under the weather
63 Troglodyte

34

TWO CENTS' WORTH   by Ed Early
Dan Blocker played the character at 22 Across.

ACROSS

1 Zoo attractions
5 Be a partner in crime
9 Windy isle off Venezuela
14 Percussion instrument
15 "Shark Tale" dragon fish
16 Kind of module
17 **Start of a popular adage**
20 More at liberty
21 Finish finish?
22 "Bonanza" character
23 Even chance
25 Brontë governess
27 Ivan or Peter
29 "Waiting to ___" (1995)
34 Clark's "Mogambo" costar
37 Well partner
40 Preserved, in a way
41 **Middle of adage**
44 Best of the lot
45 Amusing in an odd way
46 Black-maned horse
47 Most of Libya
49 Polio vaccine developer
51 Relatively few
54 Cognitive
58 Active European volcano
62 Tip off
64 Static
65 **End of adage**
68 Shine up the car again
69 Roanoke's Virginia
70 Much more than a walk
71 Applicant's aim
72 Word in a New Year's carol
73 Idiophones

DOWN

1 Astern
2 Guerrero of baseball
3 Leprechauns
4 Most cunning
5 Growler contents
6 Cookbook instruction
7 Borden bovine
8 Light brown to brownish orange
9 Styled after
10 Gordon in "Boardwalk"
11 "Once more ___ the breach . . .": Shak.
12 Expressions of contempt
13 Wonder Woman's adversary
18 Saladin's enemies
19 Not there
24 ___ Alto
26 Top-flight
28 Orange cover
30 Paul Newman title role
31 What a Persian is not
32 Capp's hyena
33 Whirling current
34 Impressed
35 Evil anagram
36 Sign in an antique shop
38 TV-show recorder
39 His teammates called him "Country"
42 Nice hot time
43 Jack in "The Rare Breed"
48 Cowardly Lion's fellow traveler
50 ___ Berry Farms
52 Pinochle declarations
53 Bronco Hall-of-Famer
55 Royal headwear
56 To one side
57 Onion relatives
58 To be, to Deneuve
59 That time
60 Eye source in "Macbeth"
61 Way away
63 Forsaken
66 Prefix for moron
67 French-born?

35 ELUSIVE CONNECTION by Larry Shearer
. . . and that connection can be found at 63 Across.

ACROSS

1 Some GI's
5 Dense ice cream
11 Duffer's delight
14 Indian tourist site
15 Danny Kaye was an ambassador for this org.
16 Patterned after
17 Handlers of stolen bonds?*
19 Racket
20 Rather
21 In a natural state
23 Peters out
26 Tear asunder
27 Kettle and Bell
30 Personal authority
33 D sharp's equivalent
35 Top-of-the-line criminal restraints?*
39 "Man-o-war on the port bow!"
41 "What's the rush?"
42 Calligraphy character?*
46 ___-Wreck
47 Dishwasher cycle
49 Outdo
50 Exclamation accompanying goose bumps
53 Strip
55 Updates machines
58 Suitable places
62 Show
63 Elusive connection in clue* answers
66 Mamie's hubby
67 Unruffled
68 Po tributary
69 Corporate component: Abbr.
70 Vacation spot
71 Dry run

DOWN

1 Boodle
2 E–J filler
3 ___-raspberry juice
4 Lebanese seaport
5 Laugh heartily
6 Cleveland–Toronto dir.
7 Vietnam Memorial designer Maya
8 Charge of wrongdoing
9 Harry Potter, for one
10 Spirit ___ Louis
11 Princess Leia's mother
12 Unfamiliar
13 Corp. division
18 "It's my pleasure!"
22 Jolt
24 "Star Trek" sequel, to fans
25 Paul Anka's "____ Beso"
27 Large city close to Phoenix
28 Daniel Mason's "____ Country"
29 Skirt feature
31 NFL stat.
32 Achieve a sensational success
34 Outstanding, in a way
36 Source
37 Album insert, informally
38 Album insert, informally
40 Taxonomic suffix
43 Ties up
44 Article in "Der Spiegel"
45 Standby maritime force, in the UK
48 Shakespearean work
50 Hair feature
51 Method of spiritual healing
52 Clergyperson's title: Abbr.
54 Fanfare
56 Gen. Bradley
57 Dieter's watchword
59 Camouflage
60 They might be tight
61 Game with 32 cards
64 ___ Paulo
65 Leb. neighbor

36 "WHERE, OH WHERE?" by John Lampkin
40 Across is an interesting clue.

ACROSS

1 Tore
6 Hot stuff
10 Knack
14 "Beetle Bailey" character
15 Amazes
16 On ___ (equipotent)
17 Indy 500 sound
18 Where the Three Little Pigs live?
20 Letter abbr.
21 Strangely
23 It can follow someone
24 SONY rival
26 Merganser features
27 Where to cry after a gutter ball?
31 Beethoven symphony "undedicated" to Napoleon
32 Bloom's buddies
33 Inc., abroad
36 Tucker
37 Sharks girl, on Broadway
39 Tend
40 Down, but with nothing to do with 3 Down
41 Flexible mineral
42 Tidy up
44 Where to kiss Big Bird?
46 Guru's quarters
49 Exchange positions
50 Bar
51 Arch preceder
53 Tee for Zorba
56 Where the Beatles made bad jokes?
58 Roof issues
60 "___ Three Lives"
61 "Vissi d'___"
62 Like "The X-Files"
63 Actor Grant
64 Adjudge
65 Chopper blade

DOWN

1 Heart song
2 Pensioner's org.
3 Grid work
4 Freudian concern
5 Devilish
6 Yes man
7 MP's quarry
8 Actual
9 "Don't ___!"
10 Ancient ship
11 "No bid"
12 Aspect
13 Lock
19 1994 Peace Nobelist
22 "Forceful" theory
25 "I cannot tell ___"
26 Comet, e.g.
27 "All ___ are off!"
28 "Mi chiamano Mimi," e.g.
29 The "A" in James A. Garfield
30 Welcome wreath
33 Poor excuse for tardiness
34 Every family has one
35 Bumper ding
38 Here, in Chihuahua
39 Links rental
41 Not fine
43 On-line seller
44 Calvados, e.g.
45 Favor
46 Jellied garnish
47 Winning 1974 Super Bowl coach
48 Sharpener
51 Lunar depression
52 A chip, maybe
54 Sony cofounder Morita
55 ___-friendly
57 Boy
59 Classified ad abbr.

37 BEATLES GIRLS   by Holden Baker

The girl asked "to play" at 27 Across is Mia Farrow's sister.

ACROSS

1 Gator's cousin
5 "Barbershop" star
9 Fawns' papas
14 Scotch mixer
15 Agnew's plea, for short
16 "To ___ Mockingbird" (1962)
17 Bruin penalty killer
18 London apartment
19 Bonehead
20 **"Wearing the face that she keeps in a jar . . ."**
23 Win over
26 Deportment
27 **"Won't you come out to play?"**
31 Spanish 1 verb
32 Confine, as farm animals
33 Rob of "The Evidence"
37 Ben & Jerry's rival
39 Carpentry grooves
41 Grime fighter
42 Steven Bochco series
44 Went white
46 "Every child. One voice." org.
47 **"Hold your head up you silly girl . . ."**
50 Weapons cache
53 Card game for two
54 **"A girl with kaleidoscope eyes . . ."**
58 Figure at a roast
59 Splinter group
60 English subway
64 Crucifixes
65 Peel
66 Sharif or Bradley
67 Rendezvous
68 Boot attachment
69 Visitor of "Deep Space Nine"

DOWN

1 CBS drama set in Las Vegas
2 Fabled bird that never lands
3 Praiseful poem
4 Life's work
5 Deduced
6 Rum mixer
7 Panache
8 Dorothy's dog
9 Giant slalom, e.g.
10 Neatness
11 Get straight
12 Geographic teaching aid
13 Nymph's pursuer
21 Reindeer herdsman
22 Pres. from Yorba Linda
23 Collectible Ford flop
24 "I ___ Lover": Mellencamp
25 Actress Hannah
28 Inappropriate
29 "Well, lah-___"
30 Paul Prudhomme's sister
34 Sot
35 "___ Joe's"
36 Trunk item
38 White, long-haired Russian dogs
40 College period
43 Most suspicious
45 Painter Anthony Van ___
48 Rembrandt van ___
49 National Aviation Hall of Fame site
50 Not foggy-headed
51 Scuttlebutt
52 "Star Trek" doctor
55 Recipe amts.
56 Jalopy
57 Off-white shade
61 Thurman in "Kill Bill"
62 Declare illegal
63 Cooperstown stat

38 PUN AND GAMES   by Matt Ginsberg
Richard Davalos played 17 Across in 1955.

ACROSS

1 Come crawling back
5 Checked for the last time
10 Lucky number in Monte Carlo?
14 Ritzy cracker
15 Santa follower
16 Dodge City lawman
17 Cal Trask's twin
18 Clip joint
19 Man of war
20 Lose focus?
23 Be constructive
24 Car bombs
25 Key contraction
27 Blood line
31 Alter egos
34 Piscine operator?
39 Odile's black skirt
41 Syrian political party
42 Head for a bar
43 Madrid water conduit?
46 A crowd, for Florence
47 Himalayan hazards
48 Fireworks sound
50 Where to find directors?
55 Big dipper's condiment
59 A matter of principal?
62 It brings people closer
63 Art supporter
64 Colored part of a ball
65 Change furniture
66 Do a make-up job
67 Go easy
68 NRA mem.
69 Checks for letters
70 Mona's surname

DOWN

1 Oak product
2 Worker who makes connections
3 Wishful thinking
4 Enclave of SE France
5 Spanker
6 "What's in ___?"
7 Having square footage
8 Collars for preppies
9 Silvio of "The Sopranos"
10 Quarantines
11 Peer group member
12 Game in the woods
13 Decorates with Charmin, briefly
21 Short highways
22 Rickman in "Sweeney Todd"
26 Massages
28 Cut-up
29 Ruler with a line
30 Mourning line
31 Half small
32 Short copy
33 Ballpark figure
35 Bit of cheer
36 Cheesecake ingredient
37 Frequent flyers stat
38 Columbus' home
40 Local personality
44 "___ She Great" (2000)
45 In business
49 Luke Skywalker's portrayer
51 Fleece
52 Bring up
53 Chicken company
54 Lost one's balance
56 The king of Champagne
57 Takes it from the top
58 Confused between ports
59 Bossy comments
60 Punch lines
61 Bath suds
62 Eva's half sister

39 OPPOSITES ATTRACT by Frances Burton
Our test solvers gave the clue at 38 Across an A+.

ACROSS

1 Juan's room
5 Pipe part
9 Eighty-six
14 Larger-than-life
15 By way of
16 Abdul of music
17 ___-do-well
18 Thought twice
20 Exams requiring no explanations
22 Scant
23 Nancy's "Rhoda" role
24 Gown's partner
27 Butch Cassidy, by birth
30 Smeller
34 Above it all
36 Unit of work
37 Bank of facts
38 Pointless college studies
42 Fail to mention
43 Follows Oct.
44 "The Age of Reason" author
45 Musical unit
46 Partygoers
49 Sun
50 Nothing
52 Troubles
54 Queries requiring no explanations
61 Baja and Sinai
62 Sword
63 Macaroni salad option
64 Poker stake
65 Hollow
66 Church officer
67 Fortnight's fourteen
68 Building wings

DOWN

1 Broadcast
2 Copycat
3 Stead
4 Realty units
5 Difficult situation
6 Louise's partner
7 Geologic divisions
8 Chew over
9 Do 50 in a 30
10 Greek prophetess
11 Old car coat
12 Pub pints
13 Launching site
19 Andy Capp's heady brew
21 Louse up
24 Chicken
25 Where Col. Travis died
26 Put forward
28 Axe handle
29 Parabola
31 Damascus, e.g.
32 Pool member
33 Artist's stand
35 Pretended
39 Americans, south of the border
40 Marker
41 Bowl over
47 Perspiring
48 Mixes a salad
51 Privileged
53 Screen out
54 Shout out
55 City in Oklahoma
56 Campus area
57 Forearm bone
58 Milky gem
59 Dudley Do-Right's love
60 Comes across
61 Edgar Award eponym

40 SHAPELY by Alan Olschwang
The Boston terrier at 26 Across was first seen in 1902.

ACROSS

1 Noose
6 Highlanders
11 Atlas page
14 McCann Erickson employees
15 Come to terms
16 Under the weather
17 Arlington landmark
19 Besides
20 Romance novelist Victoria
21 ". . . ___ I will be married to a sponge": Shak.
22 Like some interests
24 Cream puff
26 Buster Brown's dog
27 "The Graduate" plot device
33 Grad's pursuit
36 Where Hercules fought a lion
37 Sri Lankan primate
38 Province
40 Scorch
42 Kind of roast
43 Intends
45 Monte Carlo roulette bets
47 ___ vivant
48 Stock item of kitchens
51 German coal basin
52 Gasped
56 Agitate
59 Breadbasket
61 Producer De Laurentiis
62 Troy, NY, campus
63 Where it's okay to drop the ball
66 Sushi bar offering
67 Harden
68 Solecism
69 HST's successor
70 Like some stadiums
71 Makes trades

DOWN

1 Tool with a headstock
2 Impromptu
3 Olfactory offense
4 Of an atrial partition
5 Billfold filler
6 Turnstile proceeds
7 Culture medium
8 A bit of a joule
9 His papacy began in 936
10 Mali neighbor
11 Campanella had a hand in it
12 Vera's leader?
13 Trudge
18 Butterflies
23 Mexicali mister
25 Charged particle
26 Like "Macbeth"
28 Key with one sharp
29 Mortise mate
30 Chow
31 Prom transport
32 Sport's channel
33 Door part
34 Vowel-rich cookie
35 Bridges in "Norma Rae"
39 Pizzelle flavoring
41 Vents like Vesuvius
44 Inclined
46 Start-up loan org.
49 Hispanic
50 Last
53 Miss USA's wear
54 Sign up
55 They walk the walk
56 Mr. Mertz
57 Kind of column
58 Go the extra ___
59 Richard in "Nights in Rodanthe"
60 Like Goodwill goods
64 Reticent
65 Proof abbr.

LITERALLY SPEAKING by Jim Leeds
A more devilish clue for 22 Across would be "Lucifer's grandson."

ACROSS

1 Kansas motto word
7 Critical pan from an ovine member?
10 Future reading material?
14 "Absolutely certain!"
15 In progress
17 Children's nursery rhyme
19 Formed a connection
20 Montana tribe
21 Ketch kin
22 Pappy Yokum's grandson
25 Indian lentil dish
26 Mini-albums, for short
29 Chopper
31 Freshwater duck
34 Carpe diem
38 Gutter site
39 La-la lead-in
40 Photographers
42 Sticky substance
43 During
45 Oft-repeated phrase from "The Wiz"
47 Spike the punch
48 After due
49 Miss-handled
50 Spawn
52 Soviet auto
54 Former Cremona coin
58 Common site in Ft. Lauderdale
61 Reveres
64 1978 Faye Dunaway film
67 Wooden dowel used in shipbuilding
68 One of a kind
69 In ___ (actual existence)
70 Factory agent
71 Marne mornings

DOWN

1 Sufficiently
2 Tone for Stieglitz
3 Tropical fruit
4 Stores on a farm
5 Rents
6 Stub ___ (stumble)
7 Sticker
8 Folk rocker DiFranco
9 Uses an abacus
10 Church dignitary
11 Back then
12 Myanmar neighbor
13 "Damon and Pythias," for one
16 "Yipes!"
18 Dietary info
23 Maxwell Anderson play (with "The")
24 Semester testers
27 Jim and Tammy's old club
28 Basic Halloween costume
30 "I've got my ___ you!"
32 Swear
33 Economist Keyserling
34 Newcastle abundance
35 Milkseed tuft
36 Coffee additives
37 First mes of the año
41 Melbourne to Canberra dir.
44 Will beneficiary
46 Fix boundaries
51 Soon
53 Nonpro org.
55 Kuwaiti's neighbor
56 It's been seen before
57 Buffoons
58 Little bit, to L'il Abner
59 Hoity-toity put-ons
60 Yonder
62 Thing to beat
63 Endo of tennis
65 Whitewash the truth
66 Bavarian peak

42 ". . . AND NOT A DROP TO DRINK"   by Bonnie L. Gentry
Ben Affleck played 33 Down on the silver screen in 2003.

ACROSS

1 Brief words?
5 Stays for another hitch
10 Bangkok money
14 Worsted fabric
15 Wedding reception party?
16 Pigmented peeper part
17 De Gaulle alternative
18 One thrown at a rodeo
19 Be a little hoarse
20 Less than diddly
21 Enought to put you to sleep
23 "Hee Haw" humor
25 Needing to cool down, maybe
26 1973 news topic
31 Northwest's 2008 merger partner
32 "Coming to America" prince
33 "What ___ care?"
36 Capital south of Lillehammer
37 Chatty flappers
38 It's no. 1 on the Mohs scale
39 Sporty cars
40 Embroidery loop
41 City in a Porter song title
42 Slice an onion, say
44 Fundraising dinner unit
46 Wilbur's pal
47 Excellent excuse
51 Freud focus
54 Vehicle seen at a roadside diner
55 "The Audacity of Hope" author
56 Admit frankly
57 McDonald's founder Ray
58 Jordanian cash
59 Fretted fiddle
60 They move in a charged atmosphere

61 They're in control of their faculties
62 Range in "The Sound of Music"

DOWN

1 Bingo hall cry
2 "Me neither!"
3 Attendance takings
4 The Kingsmen drummer
5 A lot of summer TV
6 Long-distance runner Zátopek
7 West Coast school
8 "Fur is dead" org.
9 Shores
10 A matter of grave importance?
11 Popeye's "stop!"
12 Anyone's pronoun
13 Aquafina alternative
21 "The Sopranos" actress de Matteo
22 Apothecaries' weight
24 Mort Walker pooch
26 Mudpuppy
27 Daring exploit
28 American psychic Edgar
29 In ___ (constricted)
30 Hardly o'er
33 Matt Murdock's alter ego
34 Hispanic huzzahs
35 Zero-calorie drink
37 Liz Taylor's third husband

38 Diggs in "Rent"
40 Trodden trail
41 "Frasier" actress Gilpin
42 Earvin Johnson and namesakes
43 Imprisons
44 Prefix meaning "wing"
45 7-Up flavor
47 Glide behind a motorboat
48 Irish Rose's guy
49 "Sweater Girl" Turner
50 Supermodel David Bowie married
52 Sticky matter
53 They take night flights
56 Gardner in "Mogambo"

43 HOLLYWOOD LEGEND   by Doug Peterson
. . . and that legend can be found at 61 Across.

ACROSS

1 35th prez
4 Dolls up
10 "May I speak?"
14 Tram cargo
15 British pop star Williams
16 Danny DeVito sitcom
17 1956 epic featuring 61-A (with "The")
20 Was a straphanger
21 Signal on stage
22 Rap's Dr. ___
23 1931 crime film starring 61-A
28 Fail to see eye to eye
31 "Toddlin' Town" trains
32 "Grody!"
33 Mystique
34 Sink stopper
38 1944 film noir costarring 61-A
43 Mex. miss
44 Teensy bit
45 Novelist Kesey
46 Question starter
49 Most uncool
51 1973 sci-fi movie starring 61-Across
55 Gaza Strip gp.
56 Portuguese king
57 Goes barnstorming
61 Actor awarded an honorary Oscar in 1973
66 Minnelli of "Cabaret"
67 Kind of cracker
68 Swift bird
69 Actress Remini
70 "The Tigger Movie" character
71 Receiving line figure

DOWN

1 Writes quickly
2 Banjo ridge
3 Number-picking casino game
4 Wastefully extravagant
5 CD-___
6 Apple competitor
7 Advanced deg.
8 ___-nez
9 Inveigle
10 Chowed down
11 Ranch crew
12 Not included
13 Tightwad
18 Rum mixer
19 Repast
24 Test choice
25 Garr or Hatcher
26 Like a famous Italian tower
27 "NBA Fastbreak" channel
28 July 4th disappointments
29 Inventor Sikorsky
30 Not ajar
35 Take a shine to
36 Colorado natives
37 "Peer ___"
39 Turn on the waterworks
40 Industrious sort
41 Raison d'___
42 Traveled fast
47 Munich mister
48 Jumpy
50 A part of
51 Bit of witchcraft
52 Enduring hit
53 "Yikes!"
54 Big cat, in Córdoba
58 Played for a sap
59 "Quo Vadis" setting
60 Deliberate slight
62 Sound of contentment
63 Flat-bodied fish
64 "Just as I suspected!"
65 Limbo prop

44 "SURPRISE!" by Ed Early
Canadians will know the answer to 20 Across.

ACROSS

1 Intoxicating Polynesian drink
5 Refurbishes
10 Unpleasant amount
14 With, to Jacques
15 Notched
16 Crew concurrence
17 **Start of a quip**
20 Dollars in a "toonie"
21 Often a subject
22 Blunder
23 Topmost point
24 "Walk Like ___": The 4 Seasons
25 Tec
28 British counterpart of 4 Down
29 Playful activity
32 Barbecue morsel
33 Came home, in a way
34 Flower holder
35 **Quip: Part 2**
38 Nary a one
39 Musical wind emitter
40 Squeezed, in a way
41 Tease
42 Once again
43 Hardships
44 Dump closure
45 Hannity of FOX News
46 End of the line?
49 Jemima or Millie
50 Towel inscription
53 **End of quip**
56 ___ Blanc
57 Off-stage remark
58 Life of Riley
59 Devious maneuver
60 Destined
61 Word with fox or turkey

DOWN

1 "Critique of Judgment" author
2 Frankly admit
3 Presidential power
4 Austrian "alas!"
5 Poisons
6 Have words
7 Lawns after being cut
8 Pressure unit
9 Like some millionaires
10 Apply lightly
11 Court cry
12 "Kiss From a Rose" singer
13 Latin infinitive
18 Nightmares
19 Truckful, e.g.
23 "Get ___ on!"
24 Mentally alert
25 Neckless lizard
26 Southeast Asian capital
27 "Guten ___" ("Good evening!")
28 Macaroni shape
29 Round figure
30 Person found on the aisle
31 Requirements
33 Oft-rattled sword
34 Churchill's trademark
36 Not ready for the concert stage
37 Take off
42 On the surface of
43 Caused distress
44 LX, in Torino
45 Jacket material
46 Motorist's convenience
47 Organic compound
48 Jean in "The Da Vinci Code"
49 Working
50 Listen attentively
51 "___ many words"
52 Let it stay
54 Stars and Bars org.
55 11/11 VIP

45 EYELETS by Billie Truitt
A no-nonsense homophonic challenge.

ACROSS

1 "Get out!"
6 Deli choice
10 Cyberclutter
14 "There's ___ in the bucket"
15 Honey factory
16 Create
17 Outdoor hotel employee
18 Cools down
19 Paperless exam
20 Former Caribbean piracy center
23 Nebraska native
24 Miners dig it
25 Bribe
26 Maple drip
29 City on Lake Tahoe
31 Major suffix
33 Material for a homemade valentine
35 Bit of style
37 One who's up
38 1972 Staple Singers hit
42 Wicker willows
43 Buying binge
44 "All I ___ Do": Sheryl Crow
45 Road or young suffix
46 Take a break
50 Gobbled up
51 It lies in front of the door
53 This instant
55 Sgt. or cpl.
56 Airline seating choice
60 Opposite of riches?
62 Friend of Big Bird
63 Choppers
64 Divisible by two
65 Kind of bargain
66 Orange box
67 Part of a three-piece suit
68 Round of applause
69 Derby competitor

DOWN

1 One who delivers
2 Virtuous
3 Deodorant type
4 Out of the wind, at sea
5 "Ditto!"
6 Ultra-formal
7 Puerto ___
8 Reluctant
9 Basil sauce
10 Unhealthful air
11 Moocher
12 Rap sheet letters
13 Blanc who voiced Bugs
21 Loses it
22 News bulletin
27 Angel or Devil Ray
28 Combustible heap
30 Many a time
32 Romantic rendezvous
34 None of the above
36 1951 NFL champions
37 Mole's hole
38 Site of the earliest presidential caucus
39 Aspiring atty's exam
40 Genealogy topics
41 Drivers hear it calling
45 "A Streetcar Named Desire" character
47 Make beloved
48 Big name in lawn care
49 Long-tailed finch
52 First Hebrew letter
54 Margaret Hamilton role
57 "Money ___ everything"
58 Sign for the superstitious
59 Emperor during Rome's Great Fire
60 Lean on the accelerator
61 Forum greeting

46 ELEMENTARY by Barry C. Silk
17 Across was inducted into the Rock and Roll Hall of Fame in 2001.

ACROSS

1 Movie studio with a lion mascot
4 Happening place
9 Bone marrow lymphocyte
14 Yeoman's "Yes!"
15 Hamburger with fries, e.g.
16 Maybelline rival
17 "Bohemian Rhapsody" vocalist
19 Keep treating a black eye, maybe
20 Greek vowel
21 Prefix with state
22 Entraps
23 Take for granted
25 Palindromic time
26 1964 Presidential candidate
32 Hodges of the Dodgers
35 Traffic jam
36 The Scales, astrologically
37 "Let us know," on an invitation
39 Org.
41 Wet forecast
42 "Hello" from Hilo
44 String quartet member
46 Blushing
47 Magician of note
50 Traditional knowledge
51 Kind of photograph
55 Carve
58 Gold ingot
60 Not pro
61 Assume as fact
62 1984 Tony Award winner for "The Real Thing"
64 Napoleon's force
65 Admission of defeat
66 Dubious "gift"
67 Josh
68 Tropical ray
69 ACLU concerns

DOWN

1 Mario Puzo subject
2 Spinning toys
3 Swim competitions
4 Outfield surface
5 Standards
6 German river
7 Classic soft drink
8 Unit of work
9 Long-winged creature
10 Ionic Breeze boast
11 Arab chieftain
12 Scarf material
13 Soapmaking substances
18 Paint amateurishly
22 Old French coin
24 Bathroom rug
25 Italia seaport
27 Bail out
28 Pulitzer poet Komunyakaa
29 Uphill lift
30 Toledo's lake
31 Money in South Africa
32 Mortarboard tosser
33 Ibiza, e.g., to Spaniards
34 Ukrainian city near the Polish border
38 Steve Carlton's former team
40 Least obscure
43 One taken in
45 Bullring cheer
48 TV component
49 Strong cart
52 Reason out
53 Bikini blast, in brief
54 Thpeakth like thith
55 Cross words
56 Apple throwaway
57 West Point letters
58 Lugosi in "Ninotchka"
59 Johnny Bravo's city
62 Huck Finn's raftmate
63 NYC subway overseer

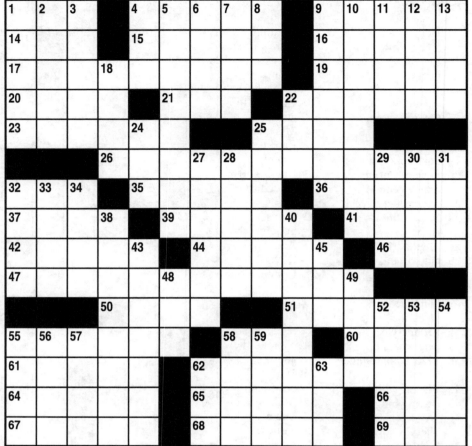

51 "CHARGE!" by Matt Ginsberg
It's unusual to find the same clue 17 times in one puzzle.

ACROSS

1 Charge
5 What Edna wouldn't give Mr. Incredible
9 Charge
13 Draftworthy
14 Boneheads
15 Charge
16 Charge
18 Graces the stage
19 Put on the feed bag
20 Bone head?
21 Dull
23 Weasel words
25 Sweeper or skip
27 Mirrored
29 Like some tires
32 Charge
35 Exert a calming influence
37 Bird from a green egg
38 Folding words
40 ___ & Perrins
41 Charge
43 Charge
44 Grosses out
47 LLD rcpt.
48 Charge
50 Without
52 Stashes away
54 Don't give this up
58 "Citizen Kane" model
60 Hurricanes' mascot
62 Kalashnikov alternative
63 Once mo'
64 Charge
67 Space (out)
68 Charge
69 High school breakout?
70 Tavern sign abbr.
71 A Dixieland quartet, perhaps
72 Redness exemplar

DOWN

1 Shoddy
2 Succeed
3 LBJ and GHWB
4 Chihuahua sound
5 Charge
6 Nahuatl speaker
7 Luau fare
8 Civic rivals
9 Went by sea
10 Charge
11 Gentle rebukes
12 Tarheel State motto word
14 Buttered up?
17 ___-garou (werewolf)
22 Dyed a robin's-egg color
24 Garry Kasparov's birthplace
26 Regular drink orders
28 Center of the Greek universe
30 Discharge
31 Charge
32 Soprano Te Kanawa
33 Moslem ruler
34 Charge
36 Charge
39 The scales of justice have two
42 Child's play
45 MDMA, familiarly
46 Man's inhumanity to man
49 Pulled down
51 JPL org.
53 Starr's 1964 stand-in
55 Charge
56 Celebrated hole
57 IQ test inventor
58 It can be purple
59 Easily bruised items
61 Wood knot
65 El operator
66 Charge

THIS AND THAT by Barry C. Silk

42 Down was a good example of a 17 Across.

ACROSS

1 Locale of many u-turns
8 Multivehicle collision
15 Chip away at
16 Glucose-creating enzyme
17 Team superstar
19 Tangles
20 Air France destination
21 Reading and others: Abbr.
22 Etching fluids
23 Clio, Erato or Urania
24 Laptop surfer's connection
25 Inarticulate pauses
26 In support of
27 Confronts
28 Total
31 Waste of taxpayer's money, usually
32 Greek for "wooden sound"
34 Habit
37 Where pawns move
41 Hard thing to swallow
42 Pain in the neck
43 Hydrocarbon ending
44 Innocent, e.g.
45 Baseball no-no
46 Used a telescope
48 Sci-fi staples
49 Legislative grp.
50 Square of Manhattan
51 Edmund Randolph was the first one
54 Cross-reference words
55 Daughter of King Minos
56 Proof goof
57 Bedroom fixture

DOWN

1 Cheat
2 Otalgia
3 Reversion
4 Took some courses
5 Ltr. accompaniment
6 Highest degrees
7 "And how!"
8 007 foe
9 Box elder, for one
10 Comrade in arms
11 Dot on a subway map: Abbr.
12 Stack found on a farm
13 Turnpike toll, e.g.
14 Keep going
18 Cheesesteak mecca
23 Japanese soup
24 Decreases in strength
26 Hanky-panky
27 Depression
29 Heavy water, for one
30 Greek singer accompaniment
31 Bookworm's counterpart
33 Signal to a road hog
34 Play the peacemaker
35 Horse for Cat Manzi
36 Informant
38 Active volcanos and earthquakes
39 Narrow, as bridges go
40 Street vendor
42 NBA great Abdul-Jabbar
45 Language group that includes Zulu
46 Spirit that's willing?
47 Figures in geometry
49 Bapt. or Meth.
50 Munich address
52 ___ hunch
53 Gallivant

57 SOUNDS LIKE by Sarah Keller
20 Across was also the site of the 1988 Summer Olympics.

ACROSS

1 Yonkers race
5 Mirror sliver
10 Some marine mammals
14 Not against
15 Free-for-all
16 "Where Eagles ___" (1968)
17 Choir member
18 Big ape
19 Garden of "delight"
20 Hyundai headquarters
22 Fabrications
23 Velvet finish?
24 Different from
26 "A Study in Scarlet" hero
30 Salami hangout?
32 Police poster pseudonym
33 Fa followers
38 It may be stacked
39 "Yes ___!"
40 Parka part
41 Motown Sound
43 Parsonage
44 Pupil's surrounder
45 Poker bluffs, at times
46 Hair goo
50 Pocketbook
51 Resident of 19 Across
52 Seafood entrée
59 Puerto ___
60 Pumping organ
61 Opening to space
62 One-third a hit by The Byrds
63 Jacques Tati role
64 Auntie of Patrick Dennis
65 Hazardous driving condition
66 Tipped at the casino
67 Small fastener

DOWN

1 " ___ the night before . . ."
2 Upset
3 NFL legend Graham
4 Gee
5 Cigs
6 Long-legged bird
7 Questionable orchard spray
8 Russo in "Get Shorty"
9 1st Fifth Republic president
10 Digger of "The Life of Riley"
11 Spokes, e.g.
12 Runnel
13 Have a feeling
21 Cask sediment
25 Entertainer Peeples
26 Derisive taunts
27 Spread in a tub
28 Stead
29 Spot for a spree?
30 Day at the movies
31 TVA output
33 "Spanish Eyes" ayes
34 Bangkok native
35 Charged particles
36 Two pills, perhaps
37 Famous Horace work
39 Deadeye
42 Central
43 Epiphany kings
45 Conquered the rapids
46 They're found at the junkyard
47 Hatred
48 Close-up lens
49 Surrounded by
50 Milton on "Texaco Star Theater"
53 Wine prefix
54 Fall short of
55 Souvlaki ingredient
56 King in a Shakespeare tragedy
57 Humorist Bombeck
58 Open-___ shoes

58 MISLEADING CLUES   by Matt Ginsberg
... and all question marks have been removed after these clues.

ACROSS

1 Office communiqué
5 RCMP's "SWAT" unit
8 China setting
12 Aweather antonym
13 Cut corners
15 "Shall we?" response
16 Slow-paced
18 Boulle citizenry
19 That fellow
20 Lacking support
22 Sidereal altar
23 Doing some knitting
25 Camel's resting place
27 Zorro's title
28 Charged swimmer
30 Emulate Demosthenes
31 Service song
33 Sign of a big hit
34 Suffix for Michael
37 Refusenik refusals
39 "Mad" people, for short
40 Hitching posts
43 Eau de Cologne
46 Like Halloween
47 Hydroxide solution
48 Book review
52 The Shirelles hit
54 Red Bull competition
56 Brick measure
57 Handle differently
59 Just scratch the surface
60 They're taken out and beaten
62 Sixty
64 Douay Bible book
65 Circulation director
66 The heavens, to Atlas
67 GE Building muralist
68 East end
69 Tableland

DOWN

1 "Chances Are" singer

2 Lily maid of Astolat
3 Ethel in "Gypsy"
4 Brit. lexicon
5 Roster ending
6 Start a new game
7 Hair piece
8 It's put before the carte
9 Become Reno-vated
10 Came again
11 Ones doing rush work
13 Bus. drivers
14 In heat
17 Support group
21 Toots of crosswords
24 Steal, ironically
26 Sung syllable
29 Finger board
32 Brief reply
33 Lab series
34 Score keepers
35 No place for a draft dodger
36 Unacquaintance
38 Play ground
41 'ard rain
42 Caboose
44 Blowholes
45 Where It.'s at
47 Work up the Dial
49 Martino replaced him in "The Godfather"
50 Wax-winged flier
51 Wright in "Track of the Cat"
53 Forgetful river
55 "___ My Mind Wander": Willie Nelson
58 Yellow line
61 Sound stage
63 Amazon end

59

FLYING STARTS   by Alan Olschwang
17 Across was "Glamour's" first redheaded covergirl.

ACROSS

1 Fences the loot
6 Cowardly Lion player
10 Stoma
14 Curve in a shoreline
15 Next to putt, in golf
16 Egg
17 Actress Everhart
18 Popular seafood entrée
20 Sewing stitch
22 Former Houston pro
23 Poisonous snake
26 Peggy or Pinky
27 Speaker's skill
29 "Old Folks at Home" subject
32 Unfounded rumor
33 Corporate chief
34 QB option
38 Awry
39 Centum start?
40 Musical speeds
41 Type of type
42 Taro dish
43 Risk takers
44 Sister series of "Merrie Melodies"
46 Spa treatment
50 Sort of serve
51 "Shanghai Noon" director
52 Pot-roast ingredient
53 Indulged in vanity
56 Excludes
58 Ladder levels
62 Play a child's game
63 Skye in "Gas Food Lodging"
64 Supplementing the hard way
65 Ripened
66 Females of the species
67 Opening

DOWN

1 S&L's org.
2 Coal holder
3 Incite
4 Not that
5 Some base runners
6 One way up
7 MP's pursuit
8 Entertain, home-style
9 Pumpernickel source
10 Set forth
11 Rounded convex molding
12 Monarch
13 A corundum
19 Elsa's reply
21 Instrument of conveyance
23 Songwriters' org.
24 Mystic
25 Terror
28 Old Olds
30 Project Galileo org.
31 Put a freeze on travel?
34 Lima's land
35 Polish the prose
36 Binge
37 Wimp
39 Belittle Winnie?
40 Dilapidated
42 Kitty
43 Added color
44 Come down
45 They're privileged
46 Great java
47 Remove a ship's supporting system
48 Device to restrict current
49 Acknowledged applause
54 Ancient alphabet character
55 Coach K's U.
57 "___ for Silence": Grafton
59 Pen point
60 New homonym
61 NCO

60 STRAIGHTFORWARD   by Ed Early
A themeless construction devoid of misleading clues.

ACROSS

1 "A ___ of robins . . ."
5 Very desirous of
13 Volcano encircling Mount Vesuvius
14 Any
16 Oust
17 Kangaroo or wombat
18 Pontiac SUV
19 Borden bovine
20 Northern ___ apple
21 "___ Mir Bist Du Schön": Andrews Sisters
22 High schooler
23 Takes a taste
24 "Let ___ Cake" (Gershwin musical)
27 Remote batteries
28 Commemorative tablet
29 Toward Des Moines, from Cheyenne
31 Evening party
32 Like many pads
33 Elevator for earls
34 Benedict XVI's office
37 Indifferent
41 Dishonor
42 Garden tool
43 Sliding screen in Japanese homes
44 Monthly expense
45 Sound of disapproval
46 Schroeder of tennis
47 "___ be my pleasure"
48 Singer Shore
49 Peru city with Inca ruins
51 Like city driving
53 Show feelings
54 Tirade deliverer
55 Nemeses
56 Generous spirit
57 Sign on a car lot

DOWN

1 Shaving-cream brand
2 Spills out the contents
3 "Peter Pan" pirate
4 Baby soother
5 Like Shoemaker–Levi's discovery
6 Checking out a tip, to detectives
7 Lines on greeting cards
8 Rose-colored dye
9 Test choice
10 Little devil
11 Causing more of a din
12 Seize and hold in a firm grip
13 "South Pacific" extra
15 French president's palace
23 Fasten, in a way
25 "Finally!"
26 Once and again
28 Waiting-room furniture
30 "___ Wednesday" (1966)
31 Command to Fido
33 Where breakers break
34 Religious community
35 Encouragement for a wrongdoer
36 Infamous box opener
37 Prescription data
38 Richard Preston bestseller (with "The")
39 Thrown out
40 Mischievous pranks
42 Vishnu worshipers
45 Door support
48 "Rats!"
49 Philippine island
50 Fringefoots
52 Course standard

61 OLD TECHNOLOGY by Pete Muller
An interesting character study by this Manhattan musician.

ACROSS

1 Select
4 Some files
9 Pay-upon-receipt items
13 Former capital of San Marino
15 Home to some cats
16 To play it you need a thin reed
17 Zambezi dweller
18 Long
19 Word with salt or land
20 They get paid
22 Child's cry
24 Drives away
26 R, 38 Across
27 Corrodes
28 New Jersey county
30 Drag queens, usually
31 Hertz rival
32 Uh-uhs
34 "Moondance" key
38 **TITLE: Part 3**
41 The ___ Ducks
42 Howard Hanson symphony
43 Greystoke's foster parents
44 "Get me outta here," on a PC
45 Talk to
47 Thou-shalt-not
50 D, 38 Across
52 Ahead
53 Fancy dress
55 Style
56 Undress with the eyes
57 East, south of the border
59 Lofgren who played with Neil and Bruce
62 Magellan's org.
63 Global warming creations
64 Little brat
65 2008 DNC chairman
66 Forearm bones
67 Bloke

DOWN

1 "Ain't 2 Proud 2 Beg" group
2 Make known
3 Asking for a hand?
4 Charles and Robinson
5 Fat Tire, for one
6 Hasty
7 August birthstone
8 N follower
9 **TITLE: Part 1**
10 Legitimate awards
11 Cruller
12 Penetrates (with in)
14 **TITLE: Part 2**
21 Costa Rican peninsula
23 Krispy ___
24 It's not usually voluntary
25 "___ got a girl for you!"
26 Amazon, for one
29 Where Wall St. is
30 Kenyan tribesman
33 Distress call, 38 Across
35 Street sign
36 "Golden Boy" playwright
37 Bowling alley button
39 "Don't worry"
40 Laser output
46 Exec. most likely to cook the books
47 You hold it for a while for interest
48 Bane of swimming pools
49 Wing wood
50 First name in mystery
51 Pampers, say
54 It's white and comes in bricks
55 It could be more
58 It can be white, black, or green
60 Infielder Merloni
61 Porky's place

ONE OF SEVEN*   by Kevin George
Opening answers to clues* relate to the title.

ACROSS

1 Poor marks
4 Balkan cars of yore
9 Place for winners
14 Casual Friday nonessential
15 Chicago film critic
16 Muse with a lyre
17 Some gametes
18 She wears bulletproof bracelets*
20 Guitar part
22 Get up
23 Frozen floater
24 Accelerate
26 Dolphin Hall-of-Famer
28 Farsi speaker
30 Expect
32 Closet type
33 Hurled
34 Dated
37 Droop
38 Corp. bigwig
40 RR stop
41 Elephant tail?
42 Draft choice
43 Cuzco natives
45 Goes without, in a way
47 "Flowers in the ___" (1987)
48 Spider's legs, e.g.
49 Joan of Arc, for one
52 First course, to Europeans
55 1998 Sarah McLachlan hit
56 Rock or Stone
58 No-win situation
61 Pluto, e.g.*
64 Bird-related prefix
65 Student/teacher, for one
66 Do penance
67 Bamboozle
68 Rub out
69 Basil-based sauce
70 Couplet

6 Mystery or horror
7 9 Across, for example
8 Holy Fr. women
9 Hardly any
10 Isaac Asimov novel
11 Japanese noodle dish
12 Like some contrasts
13 Kingdom near Fiji
19 Backpedal
21 Batman's creator
25 Nickname for Las Vegas*
27 Verify a FedEx delivery
28 "Casablanca" role
29 Yemeni money
31 Weakling
33 Centers of attention
34 Whoopi Goldberg comedy*
35 Kitty food
36 "She Done Him Wrong" star
39 Trick into wrongdoing
44 Overlay material
46 Holed out from the tee
47 Pioneering game systems
49 Mom, in Mazatlan
50 Negative campaign waging
51 Calf catcher
53 Pulling the cat's tail et al.
54 Dilfer in Super Bowl XXXV
57 How to turn on a light, perhaps
59 Proclaim
60 Brown bagger
62 Adversary
63 Auto racer Fabi

DOWN

1 Waist-length jacket
2 Lincoln's bill
3 Profound transformation*
4 Longbow wood
5 WW2 menace

63 WHERE TO FIND SOME SUPER JOBS   by Ernest Lampert
Those super jobs can be found at 17 Across.

ACROSS

1 Took a powder
7 Social worker's backlog
15 Contract term
17 Where to find some super jobs
18 Heavy-faced type
19 Most opportune
20 French poodle, e.g.?
23 Testify under oath
25 Ty Treadway, for one
26 Hibernia
27 X-ray units
31 Russian city on the Don
34 Brouhaha
36 Two-finger sign
37 Rand Corporation employee
39 Fabric fit for a king
41 Tre + tre
42 Inverness native
44 Firmly set
45 Gds.
47 Dollar rival
49 Parker in "The Great Debaters"
50 Harvard president (1933–1953)
52 Landed
53 Unmitigated
56 Melee
58 The way up a lighthouse
63 Heartfelt harangue
64 One speaking out
65 Tabloids monster

7 Vainglory
8 Public hanging?
9 "Peanuts" pianist
10 Remove, in law: Var.
11 "True Colors" singer
12 Yorkshire river
13 "___ Death": Grieg
14 Airport sign abbr.
16 Tenerife volcano
20 Sacramental oil
21 Like a cobra
22 1940s internees
24 Underpin
28 1975 Belmont Stakes winner
29 PC key
30 Placed in the Open
32 Mantra sounds
33 Weedy parcel, often
35 Guido's gold
38 Smoked salmon
40 Cooks up
43 Oater badge
46 Game similar to euchre
48 Lift
51 Broadcasting
52 "Based on ___ story"
53 In the Red
54 Tach readings
55 Blue Jay star Alex
57 Noun suffix
59 Hostess ___ Balls
60 Coolers, briefly
61 Asian honorific
62 Cyclops feature

DOWN

1 Untilled tract
2 Annie's protector (with "The")
3 B.B. King's label
4 Naughty operetta heroine
5 Ken Kesey's middle name
6 "Tarnation!"

64 SOLDIER ON   by Paula & Barry Silk
Joe Isuzu would get a kick out of solving this one.

ACROSS

1 1952 campaign name
4 Stingy person
9 "Bei Mir Bist Du ___"
14 Opposite of SSW
15 Flabbergast
16 "Common Sense" pamphleteer
17 See 37 Across
19 Nervous feeling
20 Turns on
21 Safari site: Abbr.
23 Irritated (with "up")
24 Disney collectible
25 Earth's galaxy
27 Big name in spreadsheet software
30 Konica's 2003 merger partner
31 Orbital period
32 Seeming eternity
33 Colors over
36 Blowup: Abbr.
37 Isuzu SUV
39 PC monitor
40 ___-faire
42 Decompose
43 Computer key
44 Like Iron Man
46 Land of the Rising Sun
47 Shared a boundary with
49 Minister, slangily
50 Brown, for example
51 Half a Gabor?
52 Princess topper
56 Stallone hero
58 See 37 Across
60 Bathtub feature
61 Astaire with a skirt
62 B'way notice
63 "The Playboy of the Western World" author
64 Informative
65 Sock ___ (informal dance)

DOWN

1 "Picnic" dramatist
2 James ___ Polk
3 Fed. job-discrimination watchdog
4 Subdued shade
5 Motivate
6 "Get Smart" spy agency
7 Book before Neh.
8 Hold
9 Handheld firework
10 Optimist's word
11 See 37 Across
12 Southend-___, England
13 Meshlike
18 Veggie preparer
22 Broccoli piece
25 Studied secondarily (with "in")
26 Pay stub abbr.
27 Needle holes
28 Lawless character
29 See 37 Across
30 Cattle call?
32 Goofs
34 Columnist Bombeck
35 British gun
37 Pacific, for one
38 Okra bit
41 Former California fort
43 Mayhem
45 Washington airport
46 Largest of the Channel Islands
47 Ornithophobiac's fear
48 Reproductive gland
49 Fancy wheels, informally
52 Ship's complement
53 Snack
54 Money since 2002
55 Sporty car feature
57 1988 Hanks film
59 Suffix with chlor-

65

36 ACROSS   by Jim Leeds
60 Across is a classic example of spot-on wordplay.

ACROSS

1 Rime
5 Mason's investments partner
9 Sweetened the pot
14 Cinder's remnant?
15 Suffix for oxygen
16 Mildred Ratched, for one
17 Gulf port
18 An irate Ms. Evert?
20 Ipse ___
22 Dairy case item
23 Habitude
24 TWA rival, once
26 Capek play
27 Anoint
30 Give me the tab, Mr. Donahue?
33 Menagerie
34 Fan site
35 "Oh, dear!"
36 TITLE
42 Dismantle, in Devon
43 Holocaust rescuer Sendler
44 Arrow's path
45 Greet Mr. Lauer?
51 "Sure!"
52 Volga tributary
53 "Apollo 13" vehicle
54 Like tartare
55 Hostile behavior
58 Edible agave
60 Storm troopers?
63 "The Chronicles of Clovis" author
64 Go for
65 "Hello, ___!" (Marty Allen greeting)
66 Sarah Brightman album
67 Wed
68 Meth.
69 Rose rose to fame with them

DOWN

1 Lead
2 Getting up there
3 Son of Tsar Nicholas II
4 Eastern honorific
5 Ballet's "Le ___ des Cygnes"

6 Antifreeze alcohol
7 "Madama Butterfly" matchmaker
8 Voodoo amulet
9 Fix the phone cord
10 Make like Morris
11 Amoebas, e.g.
12 Curvaceous character
13 "Jersey Boys" director McAnuff
19 Semitic house of prayer
21 Neon fish
25 "Excuse me . . ."
28 2200 hrs.
29 Fall back
31 "The Naughty Lady of Shady ___"
32 Plain-Jane
35 Early Irish alphabet
36 "Old Dog ___": Foster
37 Aesopian animal
38 Béarnaise ingredient
39 Hook, line, and sinker fishermen
40 Blood pigment
41 Them
45 Made like Rover
46 Popular bakeware brand
47 Scottish landowners
48 Pinball palace
49 Turned aweather
50 Mark and Shania
56 Dry
57 Deucy beginning
59 Narc's mark
60 Sei school
61 Boise's county
62 Rigid

66 SHERLOCKIAN SKILL by Bonnie L. Gentry
The title can be found again at 51 Across.

ACROSS

1 Bose of Bose Corp.
5 Tourney hotshot
9 Singer Stefani et al.
14 Computer file list
16 Yet to come
17 Quasimodo's love
18 Late conductor Georg
19 "Fly Away Home" bird
21 Polo crossed it
22 Short spout
23 Recreational kind of fishing
31 Steamed up
32 One voting for
33 Feeder of the Fulda
34 Check for accuracy
35 Wall paper?
39 Pastureland
40 "ER" areas
42 Theater-funding gp.
43 Old Russian oppressors
45 Pledge on the stump
49 Directional ending
50 "___ poor, wayfaring . . ."
51 SHERLOCKIAN SKILL
57 Cozy corners
58 Best Actress of 1997
60 Jezebel player of 1938
61 Preludes to operas
62 Latin for "for this"
63 Teachers' favorites
64 Get set for a shot

DOWN

1 Summertime cooler
2 Catchall abbr.
3 "Aeneid" starter
4 Simulate a historic event
5 Ballparks
6 Like wind-formed caves
7 Mother of the Valkyries
8 Cannon in "Deathtrap"
9 Commodities futures listing
10 "Yay!"
11 Some coral reef predators
12 NBA Hall-of-Famer Thurmond
13 Reagan Era prog.
15 Entered without an invitation
20 Something in your eye
23 Palindromic Honda
24 Betel palm
25 Jazz pianist Art
26 "Knockin' On Heaven's Door" singer
27 Old wheels
28 Ike's two-time opponent
29 Future viewers
30 Expunge
36 Permanent way to write
37 Takedown unit?
38 Cartoon insect superhero
41 Chat with
44 Freeway closer
46 Trig. measurement
47 Tiny squealer
48 Go-carts
51 Open to all
52 Longtime Delaware Senator
53 Breakfast restaurant chain
54 Campbell of "Relative Strangers"
55 Cologne coin
56 Sega competitor in the 16-bit market
57 Wizards and Magic org.
59 Twice, a nasty fly

67

"ZOUNDS!" by Doug Peterson
1 Across authored 86 novels and 14 short-story collections.

ACROSS

1 Western writer L'Amour
6 Bar mixer
10 Open a crack
14 "One way" indicator
15 Sign of sadness
16 Chucklehead
17 General at Gettysburg
18 Green Gables orphan
19 Black & Decker rival
20 Secure position
23 Slender swimmer
24 Foam football maker
25 Influential German school of design
27 Conduit
30 Leprechaun's land
32 Craggy peak
33 2007 BCS Championship winners
34 "Just ___ suspected!"
35 Reverberated
38 Dog bred for hunting
42 "Attention!" opposite
43 Sass
44 Actress Vardalos
45 Up to, informally
46 Spot for a nosh
47 Sea swirl
48 Err in calculating the age of
51 Study all night
53 Hubbub
54 Like the Hulk
59 Bellow in a bookstore
61 Texan's tie
62 Bright courtyards
63 "This is a disaster!"
64 Toiling away
65 67 Across's grade
66 Dozes off
67 Former frosh
68 Ford flop

DOWN

1 Heads for the hills
2 Creme-filled treat
3 Russian mountain range
4 Element found in seaweed
5 Stockholm citizen
6 Five-legged ocean dweller
7 Wine prefix
8 Waltz river
9 Bout site
10 TV interruptions
11 Engage in waggery
12 French farewell
13 Moves on casters
21 Garage lubricant
22 Ronald Reagan's nickname
26 Santa syllables
27 "Guilty," for one
28 "___ it obvious?"
29 Washington inlet
31 It has a kick to it
35 Run out
36 City near Tulsa
37 WW2 turning point
39 Placed
40 Moor's faith
41 Waterproof fabric
46 Conquistador Hernando
47 Got melodramatic
48 Wall builder
49 Neighbor of Oregon
50 Hefty horns
52 Taper off
55 Movie snippet
56 Java servers
57 Evening, casually
58 Wonka's creator
60 ___ Alamitos, CA

Some people should sing solo . . . so low that no one can hear.

ACROSS

1 Forgers
7 Turns to mush
11 Que. neighbor
14 Triumph
15 Saint Paul's sphere of influence, e.g.
17 Loves
18 Press release packets
19 Retired speedster
20 Verse weather
22 Breaks in relations
23 ___ generis
24 Protective headgear
27 Major African artery
28 Seesaw sitter of verse
30 Archenemy
32 Animator's unit
33 Ballroom dance
35 Hearty pastries
37 People who say 7 Down, seemingly
40 Dutch Guiana, today
42 Two-masters
46 Toy boy
47 Tease mercilessly
50 Stimulate
51 Snug retreat
53 Record blemish
55 Earlier
56 Sleek swimmer
58 Gettysburg general
59 Howe'er
60 Pebble Beach group
63 Out of it
65 Teflon, for example
66 Pooh pal
67 "Uh-huh"
68 Gift-getter's question
69 Howard on the back of a boat?

DOWN

1 Reuben cheeses
2 Rachel Smith's 2007 title
3 Sign off on
4 Simple ending
5 Pen
6 Ripped off
7 Sound of a self-centered singer warming up?
8 Inc., in England
9 Athlete lead-in
10 Rise dramatically
11 Pore, for one
12 Really irritates
13 Decorative dangle
16 Similar
21 Notre Dame is on one
25 Bygone leader
26 Where it's at
29 Cold War superpower
31 Light on one's feet
34 Arguing
36 "The First Time Ever ___ Your Face"
38 A wink and ___
39 Moon sight
40 Transparent, informally
41 Loosen, in a car seat
43 Sharp reprimand
44 Foghorn of cartoons
45 Moe and more
46 Hard to saw
48 FDR program
49 Cleans (up)
52 Prepared to drive
54 Palindromic principle
57 Water hazard
61 Winter product prefix
62 Crew implement
64 Favorable vote

GROUCHO SPEAKS by Ed Early

"Before I speak, I have something important to say." — Groucho Marx

ACROSS

1 Start of Paul V's papacy
5 Shirt ruffle
10 Jr. high subj.
14 "Chill Factor" hero
15 "Christ Stopped at ___": Levi
16 Abbrs. on vitamin bottles
17 Phnom Penh currency
18 **Part 1 of a Groucho Marx quip**
19 Reggae's ___-Mouse
20 Primate of Madagascar
22 Slangy assent
23 Be in store for
24 **Part 2 of quip**
27 Brazil NBA star
28 Styptic pencil ingredient
29 MLB playoff series
31 **Part 3 of quip**
35 Pre-toddler
38 Bambi, for one
39 Hit hard on the head
41 It's past due
42 Bahamas island
44 Old Mideast org.
45 Places to work out
47 **Part 4 of quip**
50 Old movie marquee name
51 Taina in "Les Girls"
52 Benzene prefix
55 Affirmation of a turndown
59 One ___ time
62 **End of quip**
65 "___ Love Her": Beatles
66 Toothbrush brand
67 Ashtabula's lake
68 Baseball's "Walking Man" Eddie
69 "___ Thy Bride": G&S
70 "From Russia With Love" killer

DOWN

1 "A League of Their Own" infielder
2 Coiffeuse's tool
3 French premier during World War 1
4 "Your silence speaks ___"
5 Nozzle
6 Detest
7 "North and South," trilogy-wise
8 "Daily Planet" photographer
9 Formal requirement
10 Server of homemade ale
11 What Harmony.com attempts to provide
12 Jack in "Call of the Wild"
13 Exams for budding attorneys
21 Rembrandt van ___
23 Feel ill
25 Fleshy fruit
26 Train car
29 "___ Without Rain" Enya
30 Canis lupis
32 Rel. to shipping
33 First deodorant soap
34 Cross inscription
36 Edinburgh hillside
37 Polite Ozark assent
39 "Love and War," trilogy-wise
40 Production batch of raw yarn
43 Nav. rank
46 Homeowner's monthly exp.
48 Absent one
49 Obi-Wan of "Star Wars"
52 On the road
53 Greek philosopher
54 Dynamic 88, for one
56 Swiss river to the Rhine
57 Norwegian speed skater Ballangrud
58 Opposite of stet
59 Microsoft Vista interface
60 Speaker of baseball
61 Befuddled
63 Stewed
64 Boating pronoun

70 MEMBER OF THE WEDDING by Barry C. Silk
26 Across was the mother of a U.S. president and lived to be 104.

ACROSS

1 Vishnu worshiper
6 LV x XL
10 Piece of glass
14 The bounding main
15 Prefix with bank or dollar
16 NYSE rival
17 "A Different World" actress
19 Prego competitor
20 Minn. neighbor
21 Tent furniture
22 Falsified a check
23 Math class subj.
24 Eliciting feeling
26 Political family matriarch
30 "___ the Roof" (1963 hit)
31 Old Testament book
32 Hosp. scan
35 "Spin City" actress
40 Grade-school trio
41 "___ Woman" (ELO hit)
42 The "I" of "The King and I"
43 Employee of Boss Hogg
47 7-Eleven drink
50 "Need You Tonight" band
51 Moorage spots
52 Upper hand
53 School dance
56 Sauce thickener
57 Member of the wedding/TITLE
60 Seaplane stop
61 New Rochelle college
62 City on the Arkansas River
63 Thunder sound
64 Having many irons in the fire
65 Bacon flavor

DOWN

1 Orange-roofed hotel, for short
2 Self-confident words
3 Brooder's place
4 Beaver's handiwork
5 Audrey Hepburn was its ambassador
6 Tryster's message
7 Hot chocolate containers
8 French vineyard
9 Playfully noncommittal
10 Equality
11 High-end violin
12 Beersheba locale
13 Radiate
18 Secluded spot
22 Canon competitor
23 Bloke
24 Carmaker Ferrari
25 Ford product, briefly
26 Essen's valley
27 Letters above 0
28 Get high?
29 "Country Grammar" rapper
32 Diner handout
33 Private, e.g.
34 "Dies ___" (Latin hymn)
36 Oodles
37 "Howards End" character
38 Shine's partner
39 Pubmates
43 Philadelphia university
44 Battle of ___ (June 1942)
45 Halo wearer, in France
46 Applies, as pressure
47 Currency substitute
48 At large
49 Throat doctor's concern
52 Many millennia
53 Panaewa Rainforest Zoo site
54 Ural River city
55 Huddle call
57 Bit of baloney
58 R&B singer Rawls
59 Bazooka, e.g.

71 ON THE LIGHTER SIDE by Matt Ginsberg
Scab or greasy spot would be an example of 36 Across.

ACROSS

1 Hook, line, and sinker
5 Flip comment
10 A crack investigator
14 Amount to be raised
15 Tiny farmer
16 Christ's following
17 Breakout
18 Stock holder
19 "Space Cowboys" org.
20 Money maker?
23 Muscateer
24 Copyholders
28 Brooks in the country
32 Pen-based
33 Short stop
36 Citrus malady?
39 Code beginning
41 Eye drops
42 Casual evening
43 Not touched up
46 Jailhouse singer
47 Lodge opening
48 Short partner
50 Fixes a clog
53 Sob sister
57 Really lie
61 Teatime for Nero
64 Spoke more than once
65 Butler's place
66 "Cheers" stoolie
67 Collars for preppies
68 Buried treasures
69 Baby bouncer
70 People with safe jobs
71 Bachelor's end

DOWN

1 Silent screen star
2 Accouter
3 Confused between ports
4 Work on moving pictures
5 Office unit
6 "What ___ mind reader?"
7 Apple for the teacher

8 Forgetful river
9 Fancy-free
10 Clubhouse "hole" number
11 Remote battery
12 IV league
13 Org. that whistled "Dixie"
21 Face of time
22 Spin backward
25 How the euphoric walk
26 One with dreads
27 Cold drops
29 Rio's follower
30 Counterfeit cops
31 Flip comment
33 Creator of cords
34 Remains barely noticeable
35 Peter and the Wolfe
37 Shout heard at the O.K. Corral
38 One of a British group
40 When people like to pay taxes?
44 English Channel swimmer
45 Chinny chatter
49 Be sneaky
51 The king of Spain
52 School board
54 Eye-catching works
55 Top of the art world
56 Abridge too far
58 Lad
59 Flight controller
60 Blow off steam
61 Invisible follower
62 Abstract ending
63 Aggravated one's condition

ISOLATIONISM   by Pete Muller
Circular reasoning may be needed to solve this challenger.

ACROSS

1 NASCAR sponsor
4 Covering of sorts
8 Sandwich server
14 Starbucks order
15 Luau dance
16 Exotic asian fruit
17 Frosted
18 See 6 down
19 180 manuevers
20 **What's inside the circles (with 38-A and 56-A)**
23 Drug quantity
24 Ont. ensemble
25 Wilma Flintstone's home
28 Calling conferences?
31 Tell on
34 Put on
35 Kirk sometimes gave it to Spock
36 Name from a Beatles' song
37 Be shy
38 **See 20 Across**
42 Vex
43 Chandler on "Friends"
44 ___ Lonely Boys (rock group)
45 Family car
46 1974 kidnappers
47 Says yes
51 Get mad
53 Ticket buyers
55 Starbucks order
56 **See 20 Across**
61 Largest S.A. country
63 Not pro
64 Tax
65 Overhauled
66 Some subdivisions
67 Before
68 Repay
69 ERA, say
70 NY puckster

DOWN

1 Boondocks
2 One who does bits?
3 It's still prevalent in the music biz
4 SeaWorld whale
5 Bears or lions
6 Red, orange, and 18 Across
7 Shows or tells all
8 Photoshop option
9 Bit
10 Hard-to-field NFL kick
11 Excited
12 Looked for a seat
13 Extra periods
21 Veg-O-Matic company
22 Gathering place
26 Political columnist Maureen
27 South Bend coaching legend
29 Searches
30 Contact, in a way
32 Nobelist Windaus
33 Fifty after
36 It may be up
38 Type of brother
39 Outlaw
40 Mixup
41 Japanese shoe company
42 Drips
47 Start of a famous quote of 1/20/61
48 The Ocean State
49 Muck
50 Fingerspeller
52 River in 61 Across
54 Records
57 Call up
58 Run away
59 Singer James
60 Tilt
61 Supporter
62 Title for A. Sharpton

73 ATTACHMENTS by Alan Olschwang
The author at 34 Across will live forever in crosswords.

ACROSS

1 He played Ugarte in "Casablanca"
6 Served sushi
9 Enjoys a sumptuous repast
14 City near Camp Pendleton
16 Bartlett of pear fame
17 Baseball crowd pleaser
19 First or last of a series?
20 Deposit-slip entry: Abbr.
21 Proportions
22 Really bad character
24 Enterprise helmsman
25 Apply oneself
29 Online journal
33 Pioneering game systems
34 "Rock On" author
36 Bruin legend
37 Giant
38 Sort of serve
39 Lenya of "Threepenny Opera"
41 Corrida cry
42 Betazoid Deanna
44 Attire
45 Costner character
47 Acquitted
49 First Earl of Chatham
51 They make galleys go
52 White man
55 Coll. course
56 Begley and Begley
59 Complete surprise
63 Stage direction
64 Duration of one orbit
65 "The Gondoliers" girl
66 ___ of Reason
67 Aussie tennis star Fraser

DOWN

1 Finish third
2 "Draft Dodger Rag" singer
3 Classic cars
4 ___ Dawn Chong
5 Nanny's triplets
6 Tightened
7 Polish prose
8 Start of a mark?
9 Steamer-trunk sticker
10 Bathing
11 Words of denial
12 Danish shoe company
13 Librarians' interjections
15 Takes a long, long look
18 Infantryman
22 Stew ingredient
23 Eye emanation
24 Loretta in "Whoops Apocalypse"
25 ___ Rouge
26 Functional
27 Phoebe in "Princess Caraboo"
28 "___ by land . . ."
30 Game of chance
31 Weed-B-Gon company
32 Frat member
35 Laurey's Aunt Murphy
38 Golf club feature
40 Expressions of wonderment
43 Gyroscope part
44 Ballroom dance
46 Treats with malice
48 Play the flute
50 Footnote word
52 Fence the loot
53 Going solo
54 Deli offerings
55 Urban blight
56 Parmenides' home
57 Twofold
58 Withered
60 Explorer Johnson
61 Sea eagle
62 "Sayonara!"

"SURPRISE!" by Ed Early

There are times when 35 Across may be more "startling" than "welcome."

ACROSS

1 It's under one's thumb
5 In hog heaven?
10 Major in astronomy?
14 Inter ___
15 Periodically repeated event
16 Pod member
17 Springs an unwelcome surprise
20 Pitching stat
21 Ever's partner
22 Sultan's edicts
23 FBI agents
24 British can
25 Heiss and Kane
28 Heartache
29 Toning targets
32 Informed
33 The D in CD-ROM
34 Blackthorn fruit
35 Springs a welcome surprise
38 1930s migrant
39 And higher, in cost
40 Mail carriers have one
41 Sparks or Beatty
42 Ballet movement
43 Bar orders
44 Strait-laced
45 Princess Margaret, to Prince Charles
46 Silence ___ (Ben Franklin pen name)
49 Magazine James Agee wrote for
50 When doubled, a Gabor
53 Springs a startling surprise
56 ___ vera
57 Hatfield or McCoy
58 Oklahoma city
59 Money in Osaka
60 Neutral one in WW2
61 Pitcher Hideo

DOWN

1 It may be stepped up
2 Having wings
3 Chaplin's second wife
4 Brit's raincoat
5 Parts of an act
6 Youngest heavyweight champ
7 Desktop image
8 Mischievous sprite
9 Fort built by Anthony Wayne in 1794
10 Standard
11 Interpret
12 Parched
13 Contributes to
18 "To be or not to be . . ." speaker
19 Pirate's potable
23 Spiny shrub
24 Fill the tank
25 Banquet entrée
26 Came to
27 The R in IRT
28 Feeling of wounded pride
29 Time traveler, perhaps
30 Showed displeasure
31 Transmits
33 Jean material
34 Imitate a peacock
36 Billie and the Fourth of July?
37 They go with Earl Grey
42 Those for
43 "West Side Story" dustup
44 Residents of Castel Gandolfo
45 Looked through the crosshairs
46 Memorable date in 1944
47 Coat-of-arms border
48 Strikebreaker
49 Tip the dealer
50 Philosopher of Elea
51 Modelesque
52 Gucci or Ray
54 "It" girl Clara
55 Multiple layer

75 OLD WEST ANESTHETIC   by Matt Ginsberg
The anesthetic can be found at 9 Down.

ACROSS
1 Big shot at a bar
5 Minn. minutes
8 Grand events
13 Eerie homonym
14 Green-headed pet
15 Woody's "Sleeper" role
16 Peer group member
17 Capital of Cambodia
18 Declaration of independence
19 "Car and Driver" features?
22 Giggly trio
23 Graphic intro
24 More to the point
27 Sale preceder
29 Rapids transit
33 Small-intestinal
34 Tearing up, perhaps
36 A new start
37 "War in the Garden of Eden" author
40 Duct opening
41 Bed material
42 Depressed area
43 Welfare state
45 TV exec Moonves
46 Fall guys
47 Bolivian bear
49 Needing some kneading
50 Five-leaved ivy
58 Trolley talk
59 In a sack
60 Commotion requiring action
61 Hurried over
62 Silly pair
63 Carries a heavy caseload
64 Dance set
65 Bisected fly
66 When people take tours in Tours

DOWN
1 Honey bunch
2 Was at the forum
3 Former capital of Italy
4 Ancestor of a text message
5 Double features
6 Axis victory
7 Baby shower
8 "Cheesy" look
9 Old West anesthetic
10 Hunter gatherer
11 Chow chaser
12 Sonic boomers of yore
14 Town's man
20 Crank up the tunas
21 Bad actors
24 Camera name
25 Ecole-ite
26 Branch headquarters
27 April ___ Day
28 Pizarro's favorite colors
30 Something to lend
31 Good chap
32 Bags it
34 Imported French wheel
35 Found under the elms
38 Clutch performer
39 Bug on the road
44 Grab some chow
46 Houseful in Britain
48 Lets the fingers do the talking
49 Piece of fish
50 Tapers
51 "___ a Song Go . . ."
52 In the pink
53 "Cool" rap artist
54 Start of a Shakespearean title
55 Keep a stiff lower lip
56 Exciting seat part
57 Flagwoman

76 SOME REAL CHALLENGES   by Victor Fleming
. . . and that real challenge can be found at 74 Down.

ACROSS

1 Gene in "Young Frankenstein"
7 Word before Mesa or Brava
12 Web auction site
16 Silent star Renée
17 Pueblo pots
18 Start of something huge
19 Birthday query*
21 Roll maker?
22 Load
23 Islands of Portugal
24 Familiar mothers
25 New Hampshire senator
27 Kind of range
28 EMT summoner
31 Signals that reflect back to antennae*
37 Be off
38 City on the Skunk
40 When the tardy arrive
41 Educ. site
42 Spanish jambalaya
44 Isle near Scotland
45 Have a yen
46 Beatitudes platitude*
50 Vino region
51 Blows away
52 Place for therapeutic magnets
53 Originally named
54 Dynamic opening?
55 ___ morgana
57 Online chuckle
58 Tanzanian capital*
61 Extended families
63 Landed
64 "Stat!"
66 Winter protection
69 ___-tung
71 Reminded
75 West Wing helper
76 Slum, e.g.*
78 Little shavers
79 "Justine" star
80 Comic Phyllis
81 Chuck
82 Cheeseparer
83 Really here

DOWN

1 Comic cries
2 Matinee hero
3 Brat Pack alum
4 Fade, in a way
5 One with electric organs
6 V-shaped fortification
7 Round at a Mexican bar, maybe
8 1993 A.L. batting champ
9 Roy Rogers' birth name
10 O'Keeffe home
11 Jonesboro campus
12 Clause separator
13 Earthwork
14 Mexican water
15 Subterranean edibles
20 Common color in heraldry
24 Mugger repellent
26 Range that divides Eurasia
27 Bleachers' shout to a batter
28 Halftime players
29 It's less than half its 1960 size
30 Wal-Mart worker
32 Burn balm
33 Carry on
34 Onetime Seminole chief
35 Corporate grade
36 Mideast money
39 "Sextette" was her last film
43 ___ Logic Corp.
44 Return letters
45 Mornings, briefly
47 "David Copperfield" wife
48 Off base?
49 Make official
54 Up until
55 To a greater extent
56 "It's ___ Unusual Day"
59 Way out
60 Highest point
62 Quarter
65 "___ say more?"
66 No-no for some dieters
67 "Ta-ta!"
68 Tacks on
69 Mid 11th-century date
70 Purposes
72 Modern addresses
73 Extra-wide shoes
74 Challenge that appears in clues*
76 "Batman" sound
77 Hullabaloo

What grocery does Bob shop at?

ACROSS

1 Melchior et al.
5 Luau dances
10 Lend an ear
16 Nobelist Pavlov
17 Japanese cartoon art
18 Records
19 Adjusts a clock
20 Passover month
21 Vinegary
22 The finest
25 Diane Renay hit "___ Blue"
26 One married to the mob
30 Kind of kick
33 Oenophile's concern
35 Guesstimate words
36 Fatso
38 Shade provider
40 Thumbs-up
41 Chi Omega mascot
42 Like a starched shirt
43 Always, in verse
44 Cold-shoulder
46 Thwart
47 "___ a Long Way to Tipperary"
50 Harper Lee character
52 Former California fort
53 Kind of artist
54 Horrified
56 "Photoplay" photos
59 Maui mementos
60 A deadly sin
61 Matlin in "Walker"
62 ABC's of a successful pangram?
65 Medical breakthrough
66 Charles Henry Phillips product
72 Go back
75 Affair
76 "Cheers" regular
77 Eats up
78 Important exam
79 "The Time Machine" people
80 Vespas
81 Steps over a fence
82 Cub Scout groups

DOWN

1 Catchall abbr.
2 Allege as fact
3 Ticket info
4 Madness
5 Home of Dartmouth
6 Amalgamate
7 Tilt, at sea
8 Nanking nanny
9 Dakar is there
10 Live's partner
11 Disguised, briefly
12 Blended family members
13 Asian holiday
14 "___ tu" ("A Masked Ball" aria)
15 White House advisory grp.
23 Earned
24 Lightning McQueen, e.g.
27 Like orchids
28 Clairvoyance
29 Hobbs of "The Natural"
30 Instrument in a wind quintet
31 Microwave, slangily
32 NCC-1701 is one
33 Sign of boredom
34 Building addition
37 Fight card unit
38 Dernier ___ (the latest thing)
39 Be indisposed
42 ___ of Hammurabi
44 "Mayday!"
45 QB's cry
46 Stew
48 Bit of filming
49 "Peter Pan" pirate
51 Sweater material
52 Quaker Oats cereal
53 Checked baggage
54 Cookbook phrase
55 Do goo
56 Some jeans
57 What rumrunners do
58 Bring home
60 Albanian currency
63 Helped
64 Give a benediction
65 Root ___
67 Dart about
68 "Austin Powers" character ___-Me
69 Matchless
70 Niblick, for one
71 "Lucky Jim" author
72 Dodge truck
73 Tokyo, once
74 Lift

LOATH OATHS   by Patrick Jordan
58 Across was created by Pulitzer Prize–winning cartoonist Jeff MacNelly.

ACROSS

1 Grocery shelf lineup
5 Urban areas, slangily
10 Most leafless
16 Magnetizable metal
17 First symptom
18 Kind of bet at Belmont
19 Venus de ___
20 Landlord's document
21 Whitney's "The Preacher's Wife" costar
22 **Start of a quip**
25 "I'll take the offer, Howie!"
26 Pres. of the USA
27 Rod hidden by hubcaps
28 Conceded putt
29 Adjective for a slum
33 Rooster's weapon
35 Firth of Clyde port
36 Filling station fixture
37 Helpful hints
40 The Venture in "King Kong," e.g.
42 Wimbledon shot
43 **More of quip**
48 Airy courtyards
50 Ginger or pale follower
51 Deerstalker projection
52 **More of quip**
57 Wield diligently
58 Purple martin of the funnies
59 Nitwit
60 Loud laughter or thunder
61 OutKast's genre
64 "Disappear" band
66 Ruthless rule
68 Blow away
70 Jack in "The Comancheros"
73 Lyndon's female beagle
74 Beguiling trick
75 **End of quip**
80 Authorize
83 "Hollywood" author Gore

84 "I, Claudius" outfit
85 Disposed (of)
86 Alpine ridge
87 Tear's partner
88 Hall of fame candidates
89 "A thing of beauty . . ." poet
90 18-Across payout factor

DOWN

1 Hendrix at Woodstock
2 Operatic number
3 Dicer's turn
4 Alp topper
5 Ise or Mecca, e.g.
6 Singles
7 Expo '70 site
8 Spay or neuter
9 Fills with resolve
10 Spot to sack out
11 Hewing tool
12 Brooks in "Cop"
13 Itchy skin problem
14 Like a romance novel
15 Superior in stature
23 Feel poorly
24 Soda aisle brand
28 Express sorrow
29 Paintball field sound
30 "___ the raven . . ."
31 Shadow's middle
32 Tango move
34 Hesitant syllables
38 Recite the Hail Mary
39 Hardly hollow
41 Chi-omega link
43 Driving club
44 Meeting reminder, perhaps
45 "Quaking" tree
46 1992 Rangers retiree Ryan
47 With a straight face
49 "___ been real!"

53 Outpaced every opponent
54 Sinister spells
55 Nimble-minded
56 Apertures for some voyeurs
60 Sequel's subtitle, often
61 Cake mix additive
62 Tchaikovsky's "Piano Trio in ___"
63 Wine taster's asset
65 Language akin to Czech
67 TD signaler
69 Serengeti grazer
71 Engulfed in flames
72 Princess in the Golden Fleece myth
76 Horsepower fraction
77 Went after weeds
78 Quaint "Yikes!"
79 Its moons are Phobos and Deimos
81 Squiffed
82 MSS markers

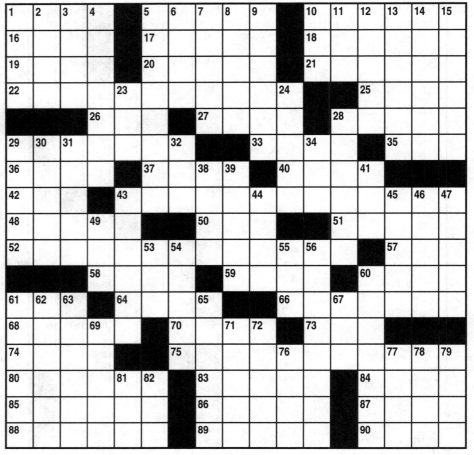

79 UNDERCOVER FORCE   by Chase McFarland
Can you uncover this undercover force below?

ACROSS

1 Extend an invitation for
6 "Poor me!"
10 Deep-dish dish
16 Sports show ending
17 Popular techno musician
18 Bearing red tags, maybe
19 Point a finger at
20 It won't let you be objective
21 Initial
22 Lima founder
25 Auto of old
26 ___ the crack of dawn
27 High-school subj.
28 Exes with joint custody
33 Crunch targets
35 "Just ___ am, without . . ."
36 Constellation near Norma
37 ___ es Salaam
38 Savage
40 Deep-red apples
43 On the agenda
45 Goes for the passer
49 Gallup product
52 Salon worker
53 Reagan cabinet member
54 "Pagliacci" role
55 Keach or Lattislaw
57 Cruise or Mix
59 Party member, briefly
60 Soft shoe
63 "Baudolino" author
64 Swimming pool game
67 Small batteries
69 Child support?
71 Flight board abbr.
72 They ended with the Peace of Callias
78 13th-century Italian sculptor
79 Breakfast acronym
80 "___ the Tiger" ("Rocky III" song)
82 Pouting
83 Etta of old comics
84 Mil. rank
85 It gives you an out
86 Huxtable and Lovelace
87 "Whole ___ Shakin' Goin' On"

DOWN

1 Wall St. maven
2 Philosophical concept
3 Reliant or Aries
4 2004 Emmy nominee Braun
5 Can tail?
6 Both up front?
7 Trixie Flagston's mom
8 Item with beads
9 Computer bulletin board administrator
10 Red board?
11 "Il Trovatore" role
12 Tavern sign abbr.
13 Pro ___ (for one's country)
14 Oldmobile models of 2000
15 Essence of orange blossom
23 Like Davidson College
24 Steve Allen successor
28 Quibbles
29 "Are you in ___?"
30 Namby-___ (silly)
31 Brussels-based alliance
32 The Heisman, for one
34 Kind of double
38 "La Isla ___": Madonna
39 Hockey's Phil, familiarly
41 Some pipe joints
42 Spanish dice roll
44 Noche follower
46 John Havlicek's nickname
47 Eero's father
48 Camera technique
50 Whimsical eccentrics
51 Sikorsky or Stravinsky
56 Scoop site
58 Thom of footwear
60 Chatterbox
61 Crew action
62 Salad type
64 Worked as a combination
65 "Animal Farm" author
66 Invoke
68 Land's end?
70 Eleniak of "Baywatch"
73 Till compartment
74 Kappa preceder
75 Studios, maybe: Abbr.
76 Four-sided fig.
77 Hearth buildup
81 Boca's st.

80

JUDGE DREAD   by Bonnie L. Gentry
"You know you've had a bad 'Idol' performance when . . ."

ACROSS

1 Out on a limb
6 "Are you game?"
12 Suspicious of
16 Bob's partner
17 Is nuts about
18 Cut with a scythe
19 **Simon says . . .**
22 Reclined
23 Unagi, at sushi bars
24 One making shrill barks
25 Like wee-uns
26 "Got it!" concordance
30 Massey of old films
31 Pioneer in close-up magic
33 Gun stock
35 Whitaker's costar in "The Crying Game"
36 Athletic shoe feature
37 Solomonlike
40 Gangly one
43 Tibetan milk source
44 Congressional creation
46 JetBlue competitor
47 **Randy says . . .**
51 Catch, as a perp
52 It can be seen during el día
53 Part of UNLV
54 Opie player
55 Exile site for Napoleon
57 Half-speed, e.g.
59 Sighing sound
60 Affront to neighbors
62 Governing bodies
66 Prospectors' discoveries
68 Justifiable
70 Two halves
71 Go into banks, perhaps
73 "Yoo-___!"
74 Parks of civil-rights history
75 **Paula says . . .**
80 1986 Peace Nobelist Wiesel
81 Move to the front row, maybe
82 Solicitous phrase
83 Part of a microscope
84 Have a one-track mind
85 Destroy, as documents

DOWN

1 Riding-wear fabrics
2 What one doesn't pay at a clearance sale
3 Without breaking a sweat
4 "The Blackboard Jungle" author Hunter
5 Wilmington's st.
6 Greet silently
7 Writer St. Johns
8 ". . . ___ a lender be"
9 Give 100%, say
10 Word in William Shatner titles
11 First words to stand for
12 Tribal precepts, by and large
13 Palo Alto–based IT network
14 Already spoken for
15 Phantom's milieu
20 Hotelier Helmsley
21 Hold back Cupid
26 Encirclements, of sorts
27 1995 Batman portrayer
28 Middle of a famous palindrome
29 "Magic Hour" novelist Susan
32 Select at random
34 Design with acid
36 Mushroom topper
38 Pieced together
39 Nervously irritable
40 "Same Old Lang ___": Fogelberg
41 Santa's revenge
42 Said "nyah, nyah, nyah"
43 Coward's color
45 Bossy boss
48 Katharine in "Shenandoah"
49 Confucian "way"
50 Capital east of Riyadh
56 Responses to bridge bids?
58 Element below plata in the periodic table
59 "Facetious" fivesome
61 This, to Cervantes
62 Piglets
63 Out-of-bounds, so to speak
64 Nutrition shake brand
65 Tamper-resistant
66 RCA or EMI
67 Seed structure
69 '89 World Series winners
72 Overseas union unit
74 In clover
76 Civil War soldier
77 Pluralizer, often
78 Sacramento newspaper
79 Frank McCourt novel

81 BROKEN PROMISES by Patrick Jordan
The five-letter answer to 5 Across is not TENOR.

ACROSS
1 Scout's badge holder
5 Barbershop quartet member?
10 Seal of approval
16 Quarterback's cry
17 Bother greatly
18 Talk over again
19 Novel notion
20 Asian palm
21 1804 Beethoven symphony
22 Plush bed or sofa item*
25 Did in
26 Oceanarium wrigglers
27 Ingenue's quality
29 Like an epigram
31 Stern lecture tool?*
35 Buck or sock add-on
36 British leaders, briefly
39 Submit taxes online
40 Meditative sect
41 Crop-menacing insect
44 Concerns for fashionistas
45 Ed Sullivan's "Toast of the Town," e.g.*
47 Receive willingly
50 Closed (in on)
51 **Promise broken in clue* answers**
54 Base manned by I Don't Know
55 Make the last payment on
56 "Heartburn" author Ephron
57 "The Blackboard Jungle" actor*
62 Quick kisses
63 "My bad!"
65 Beyond, at first?
66 Provide a cure for
69 Lava stream*
73 Thrill
75 Brother of Moses
76 "___ Rose" ("Music Man" tune)
77 Written reminiscence
78 Had a go at
79 Polo Ralph Lauren rival
80 Script segments
81 Weensy preceder
82 Gen-___ (boomers' offspring)

DOWN
1 Gangster's knife
2 Errand runner
3 Anatomy class display
4 Dismissal, slangily
5 Auditorium array
6 47-stringed instrument
7 Finished some leftovers
8 Former Czech president Havel
9 Plus others, in Pliny's day
10 Twisted woolen yarn
11 ___ Lingus
12 Elite group
13 Car-denting stones
14 Verb suffix
15 Spring phenomenon
23 1960s TV action star Ron
24 Lacto-___ vegetarian
28 Steering arm attachment
29 Candy in collectible dispensers
30 Ticked-off feeling
32 Storage crib
33 GOP member?
34 Bullets legend Unseld
36 Freighter's destination
37 Long-distance inits.
38 Canal opened in 1869
41 What a Newfoundland isn't
42 Sault ___ Marie
43 Veteran's counterpart
44 At which point
45 Brilliant red
46 Piglet parent
47 Off-road vehicle
48 X, to Xenophon
49 Title for JFK or LBJ
51 Compete on "American Idol," say
52 Sitcom planet
53 "What ___ I thinking?"
56 Blockbuster rival
58 Nomadic types
59 One of Pooh's pals
60 Recently
61 Message in a corporate image ad
62 Chest muscle, for short
64 "Beyond the Sea" subject Bobby
65 She honeymooned on 52 Down
66 Some alteration targets
67 Major suit?
68 Gadget company of cartoondom
70 Refusals
71 Gas leak evidence
72 Gum globs
74 Casting vote's cause

AFTER ALL* by Sam Bellotto Jr.

22 Across is now a national park on the Bristol Channel coast of England.

ACROSS

1 He's a good feller
6 Porks off
11 Redd of "The Royal Family"
15 Crystal-lined rock
16 Dotty
17 "Enquirer" blurb
18 Stevie Wonder hit of 1973*
20 Lady of Seville
21 E-mail chuckle
22 "Lorna Doone" setting
23 YouTube offerings
25 "Storms in Africa" singer
27 Rocky pinnacle
28 Sooner than
29 Police band broadcast*
36 Star on Sirius
38 Pelouze product
39 "There will ___ laughter": Orwell
40 Centennial number
41 "The Cyclops" has just one
43 NPR's Glass
44 Comic from Copenhagen
45 Shakespeare play that opens in Rousillon*
49 Make a new bow
50 Pet
51 Son of Gad
52 Match, in a way
53 LAX guesstimates
54 Nonsense
56 Perceptions
58 1989 Don Bluth animated film*
61 Sale word
62 Road-map abbr.
63 Dial abbr.
67 The Mishnah is part of it
70 Sawhorse, basically
73 Prefix for biology
74 Arthur of "Hoop Dreams"
75 Like many a winning vacation package*
78 Esfahan coin
79 Duo, plus five
80 Actress Sokoloff
81 Conservative Party predecessor
82 "Things We Said ___": Beatles
83 Terry or Drew

DOWN

1 Mentally acute
2 Element 54
3 Shannon or Parker
4 Fanfare
5 Glacial snowfield
6 Snowbirds' meccas
7 Dope
8 Polygraph flunker
9 New Haven student
10 Truckling
11 Cheese-knife type
12 Sioux speaker
13 One of the phobias
14 Present day?
16 "American Idol" judge
19 Like the thylacine
24 "___ be darned!"
26 Bonobo
28 Where Gingrich got his PhD
30 Alb covering
31 GPS units, iPods, PDAs, etc.
32 Without a stitch
33 Rosie O'Donnell's middle name
34 Fireplaces
35 Popular British TV actress Gordon
36 Orlando Pirates home
37 Digital ID?
40 "And the wine ___": Psalms 75:8
42 Reporter's end
44 "Penny Lane" was on this
46 Not at all clumsily
47 Buck's tail
48 "You ___ crazy!"
54 Most near absolute zero
55 Bully on "The Simpsons"
57 Roxy Music's Brian
59 Wildebeest
60 Nautical call
64 Janis Joplin album
65 Relegate
66 Winged Godzilla foe
67 Open pie
68 Financial allowance
69 "All in the Family" producer
70 Given the O.K.
71 Spanakopita cheese
72 Farmer Hoggett's wife in "Babe"
76 Banh ___ (Vietnamese crepe)
77 NTSC alternative

83 ENCORE PRESENTATION by Victor Fleming
50 Across may be a good place to start solving.

ACROSS

1 Suburban additions?
5 Frond growers
10 Memory-filled spans
16 Go squishy
17 Village ___
18 Source of Tiger's frustration
19 Not in balance*
21 Like some hot desserts
22 Basket twigs
23 Hop and jump partner
25 Fudd of toons
26 Some stanzas
28 Langley initials
30 Embitterment
31 Forestry units
32 Paid expenses*
37 Writer Tarbell
38 Goes it alone
39 Tended
44 Places for patches
46 Chinese hard-liner
49 Find repugnant
50 TITLE, WHEN ENCORED*
52 Inclination
53 Beyond acceptable limits
55 Ventimiglia of "Heroes"
56 Company with a blue globe logo
57 Renaissance instruments
59 "Hinky Dinky Parlay ___"
60 In uncomfortable surroundings*
63 Is adjacent to
68 ___ cit. (footnote abbr.)
69 "___ Night Like This": Dylan
70 One who's out early
72 Atoll
75 Globule
78 Showed shortness of breath
79 Formal fiddle
81 Hardly competitive*
83 On or before deadline

84 Kind of roll
85 Sculptor Nadelman
86 Mortified
87 Good feature
88 U.S. hwys., e.g.

DOWN

1 Duty
2 In fewer words
3 Ava's role in "Mogambo"
4 Fla. beach spot
5 Leading the pack
6 Early autumn setting in Cambridge
7 "How the Other Half Lives" author
8 Dinette spot
9 Yule visitor, briefly
10 9 Down helper
11 Profusion
12 Iridescent stone
13 Not available*
14 Golfer Green
15 Cordwood measures
20 Miner's quest
24 Some charts
27 Prefix for gyra
29 Quark's place
33 Disrepute and then some
34 Like some audiences
35 Seize
36 Alley Oop's love interest
39 Made use of a sedan
40 Blood-typing letters
41 Fictitious*
42 Silken and firm, e.g.
43 Pontificate
45 Wise old head
47 Recovery place
48 Pro ___

51 Civil War authority Shelby
54 Move, realtor-style
58 Mail off
60 "Twelfth Night" countess
61 ___ around (prying)
62 First first lady
63 "Do you have Prince Albert in ___?"
64 Headline
65 Adjust, as the level of a projector
66 ___ Beanie Babies
67 Swamp grasses
71 Rush
73 Oscar-winner Kazan
74 Rice and Robbins
76 Cries of discovery
77 Writes
80 Divided court feature
82 Tommy who sang "Jam Up Jelly Tight"

84 JAVA DEVELOPMENT   by Kevin George
Matt Ryan was a 68 Across in 2008.

ACROSS

1 Glass of NPR
4 Sudden hirings and firings
11 Gushing flattery
16 Crew need
17 Phrase heard during a police raid
18 Stun gun
19 Coven concoction
21 Curly hair or freckles
22 Further
23 Swell
24 Simon and Diamond
25 Entrée at the Friars' Club?
31 Exercise form
34 "___ Mine": Beatles
35 Difficulty
36 Top-secret grp.
37 ___-Lucia Cortez of "Lost"
38 Mementos
41 Same old, same old
44 Omelet ingredient
45 Chinese: Prefix
46 Legal claim
48 Just one of those things?
52 Jersey cager
55 Behave appropriately
58 Change place?
62 "Mazel ___!"
63 French way
64 Instructional material?
65 German 101 article
66 Descendant of both Madrid and Mongolia?
68 Elite draftee
72 Transported
73 Mai ___
74 Mid-month time
78 Petrol unit
79 Badly bludgeon
83 Al Yankovic hit that went gold
84 ___ Field Airport, nka O'Hare
85 ER pronouncement
86 Hebrew leader?
87 Number one

88 "___ for Silence": Grafton

DOWN

1 Spirit Lake locale
2 Poker table perimeter
3 They can be liberal
4 Educ. institution
5 Ground breaker
6 Colorado NHLers
7 Stick-y meals?
8 Bug
9 1957 Oscar winner Miyoshi
10 Seat of worship
11 Ávila saint
12 Star of many Nintendo games
13 For fun
14 Publish anew
15 Clubber Lang portrayer
20 Chanel of fashion
24 Echo, for one
26 Silicon Valley auctioneer
27 Suffix with duck or seed
28 Online greeting
29 Push
30 Superstation letters
31 Added stipulations
32 Morales of "Vanished"
33 Drought relief
38 Criticize
39 Menu choice?
40 Qtys.
42 NFL Hall-of-Famer Howie
43 Neighbor of Pakistan
47 Tally
49 Mata ___
50 Fuego fighter
51 Prom attendee

53 White canines
54 Retro Ford of 2002
56 "Me neither!"
57 Emergency order, briefly
58 Adobe Reader file
59 Primary
60 Strangler's weapon
61 It has 12 meses
66 Piaf and Wharton
67 Pass over
69 Type of mall or steak
70 In ___ (unborn)
71 Springarn Medal org.
75 Threads
76 Morlock victims
77 Resting places
78 Open field
79 Droid
80 Select
81 Spanish Main cargo
82 Home security company

85

" 'S WONDERFUL!"   by Jay Sullivan
19 Across is a Scary clue!

ACROSS

1 Unwanted growth
6 Caped Crusader's domain
12 They have teeth in them
16 Some fellers
17 Wing it
18 "I was afraid of that!"
19 Where "Wannabe" gets a lot of air time?
21 Remote possibility
22 Melisande's lover
23 Kind of will?
24 Spring part
25 Sordid
26 Mast?
28 Wavy area
29 Overnight letter
30 Yellowfin tuna
31 Newton's ___ of motion
34 Overhead item
36 Serengeti sight
38 They have pull
42 Milo of the movies
44 The price you pay
46 Nonstop
48 Words of praise
49 Batting .200?
52 Just deserts
53 View from Maui
55 An Ivy Leaguer
56 Serviceable
58 Punjab separatist
59 Yolk container
61 Treebeard's doc?
63 One whose business is taking off
64 It could be toast
66 Swiss sight
68 Sancho Panza's mount
70 Candy store?
74 Hire all new actors
78 Like some AA batteries
79 NATO mbr.
80 Eroded
81 Fox fave, familiarly
82 Crew's cruise?
84 Went downhill

85 It's more than a promise
86 After lunch, perhaps
87 "The Eagles" cofounder
88 Familiar with
89 Less loco

DOWN

1 Social insects
2 Boot out
3 Nellie's "South Pacific" lover
4 Formerly chic
5 Blessed event?
6 Some heaters
7 Fertilization sites
8 "Assumption of the Virgin" painter
9 Coming down hard
10 Coral construction
11 Chess group
12 Spunk
13 Enterprise officer
14 Recurring theme
15 Book store
20 Physician's request
24 Butt end
26 Long-necked lute
27 Hot spot
31 Impends
32 Likewise
33 Large gastropod
35 Places in the heart
37 On order
39 Go figure
40 Stir up
41 Display disdain
43 Stock quote
45 Luck of the draw
47 From ___ Z

50 Where to pick up dates
51 Took time out
54 "Is that so?"
57 Il Duce follower
60 Take prisoner
62 Paris pie
65 Since Jan. 1
67 Dilly-dallied
69 Regards
70 Catch wind of
71 Dentist's request
72 School of Paris
73 Andy in "The Devil Wears Prada"
75 It's not free of charge
76 Old age
77 It's in development
80 Regards
82 Apt name for a cook
83 GPS measurement

86 BLUE MATERIAL by Richard Silvestri

Words spoken by Ariel in "The Tempest" inspired the composition at 15 Down.

ACROSS

1 Wore a hole in the rug
6 Whirlpool alternative
11 Little bit of scat
16 Wide open
17 Corporate division
18 Sovereign
19 Put the check in the mail
20 Snow removers
21 Quaker in the forest
22 "Happy Birthday" writer
24 **Start of a question**
26 North Star
29 Using few words
30 Bass organ
31 Home-based hardware
33 Somewhat
34 Run for fun
37 Brewpub order
38 Vectors' counterparts
40 Mountain lion
41 In memory
42 Column type
44 **Middle of the question**
48 Bud
49 Camden Yards player
50 Level
51 Auto annoyances
53 Feathery accessory
56 Homer Simpson's father
57 Tenant organization
59 Blazed a trail
60 "Bang a Gong" group
61 Like 37 Across
63 Call for
65 **End of the question**
70 Run a rag around
71 Subside
72 "Silas Marner" author
74 The Jetsons' dog
77 Moon vehicle
78 Right-hand page
79 Coast condition?
80 "Nancy Drew" author
81 Imbue
82 Neighbor of Ethiopia

DOWN

1 72, often
2 Get better in the cellar
3 Garbo role
4 Heroic
5 Discourage
6 Egyptian cobra
7 Where Timbuktu is
8 In the air
9 It's rung in
10 Categorizes
11 Found a caller
12 Step on it
13 Brand that goes to the dogs
14 Onion's kin
15 "Where the Bee Sucks" composer
23 Skydiver's line
25 Ryder Cup team
26 Major golf tourney
27 Upton Sinclair novel
28 Muffler
32 Passel
34 2007 Ellen Page film
35 Persian poet
36 Sal, in the song
38 Bowl over
39 Kind of committee
40 Accumulation
41 Hook's helper
42 Took to task
43 Office seekers
44 Kaffiyeh wearer
45 Tailor's concern
46 Sea east of the Caspian
47 Floor worker
48 Monastery address
51 Cads
52 Shoulder piece
53 "Billy Budd" composer
54 Poetic preposition
55 Bunyan cutter
57 Stick together
58 Area code preceder
60 Melee
62 Supermarket marking
64 Canvasback comment
65 Gloomy
66 Orchestral reed
67 Roof feature
68 Tommy's gun
69 Make an entry
73 Do better than
75 Bit of sunshine
76 Feast-famine filler

87 HIDDEN RIFT by Billie Truitt
A puzzle that's a bit cracked.

ACROSS

1 U-bend under a sink
5 Clothing
11 Award of Valor org.
15 Circle dances
17 Like clothes in a hamper
18 Bring in
19 Low-tech calculators
20 Dream up
21 Bach's "Mass in ___"
22 Phrase seen on a vending machine
24 Excessive
26 Hold contents
27 German industrial region
29 Trojan War epic
32 Signs of relief
33 Store door
36 Day-___ paint
37 Doo-wop syllable
38 U.S. Open tennis stadium
39 Take a taste
40 Mary-Kate or Ashley
42 Pre-1917 monarch
45 Stairwell sounds
47 Cheer heard at a Nittany Lions game
50 Spicy Southern stew
53 ___-bitty
54 Horseshoe-shaped letter
58 Unrefined find
59 Ceremonial splendor
61 Just average
63 Ticked off
64 "May it never be!"
68 Installments, briefly
69 Kind of pointer or tag
70 Jekyll's alter ego
71 Queen of daytime TV
73 Totally lost
75 Create a rift/PUZZLE TITLE
78 Sugar lump
80 One-dimensional
82 Mark the end of ___
83 "___ do you good!"
84 S.O.S. alternative
85 Exorbitant
86 Kiter's holding
87 Welcomes warmly
88 Merrie ___ England

DOWN

1 Compared to
2 Telemarketer's tactic
3 Plains native
4 Indiana cagers
5 Fungal spore sacs
6 Bull-fighter
7 Jams
8 Dockers' gp.
9 Election-night data
10 First lady's garden?
11 Interstellar cloud
12 Inherited
13 Jackie's second
14 Raggedy doll
16 Croon or warble
23 Have a snack
25 MGM lion?
28 "Citizen Kane" model
30 It can be a lot
31 Onetime Tunisian rulers
32 In the past
34 Abominate
35 "Take ___ Train"
37 Busybodies
41 Bird of the future
43 Short-tempered
44 Hill dweller
46 Clothing line
48 Pal of Christopher Robin
49 Proofreader's find
50 Seethe
51 Major in astronomy?
52 Not throw-away
55 John Steed's partner
56 Collected
57 Pop-ups, e.g.
60 Angora sweaters
62 Yours, to Yvette
65 Go over again
66 Ford flops
67 Sherpa, perhaps
68 Right away
72 School support gps.
74 Isle of exile
76 Scientology's Hubbard
77 Collar location
78 Geometric fig.
79 4 x 4, for short
81 An end to peace?

88 BLANK EXPRESSIONS by Jill Winslow
That's not a misspelling in the answer at 19 Across.

ACROSS

1 Concert piano
6 Scratch target
10 Aftershock
16 CSA general
17 Vicinity
18 Halcyon
19 **With her marriage she got ___**
22 Kwanzaa mo.
23 Long-legged wader
24 Airplane, for short
25 Mr. Jinks, for one
26 Verb suffix
27 Form W-9 info
28 Former Cosmo great
29 **Stiff the exorcist and ___**
36 French department
37 Lena in "Romeo Is Bleeding"
38 D-Day craft
39 Laughter units
41 Flagstick
42 It can hold its liquor
43 007's "GoldenEye" car
46 **What's the definition of a will? (___)**
50 Go follows it
51 "You got it!"
52 Fishing essential
53 Get in the net
54 Org. with a motto
55 Not belonging to others
56 Flying pest
57 **Shotgun wedding: A ___**
63 Come close
64 R. Shapiro, notably
65 Wriggly swimmer
66 Spring runner
67 In good health
69 Show satisfaction
71 "What guy?"
74 **A chicken crossing the road ___**
78 Must
79 First name in architecture
80 Crown
81 Most peculiar
82 Dog food brand
83 Book of Mormon book

DOWN

1 Alum
2 Descartes
3 Baldwin in "Pearl Harbor"
4 Not a rerun
5 Bond girl Richards
6 Branches
7 God struck by a spear in "The Iliad"
8 Great white hunter milieu?
9 Stays in there
10 Bygone ruler
11 Fix up
12 Commit a no-no
13 "I hate those ___ to pieces!": Mr. Jinks
14 Discounted
15 Finished the defense
20 Help out
21 Unpleasant sounds
26 S-curves
27 Ocean spray
28 Calif. hrs.
29 Mystical people
30 Take the podium
31 In the dark
32 Ring boundaries
33 Charles Lamb
34 Eastern European
35 Rob in "Nostradamus"
40 Definitive word
42 India.Arie hit
43 "___ Devil" (first 3-D film)
44 Friend of Robespierre
45 "Christina's World" painter
47 Like Marlee Matlin
48 Out of the picture
49 Helpful one
54 Put money down
55 Raised to a bishop
57 Place to 54 Down
58 Lowered in prestige
59 Put away a dish at night
60 "Wild Hogs" director Becker
61 Enlarge
62 Take down a peg
67 Beach shelters
68 Heaps
69 Hoopoe, e.g.
70 Son of Seth
71 Accompanied by
72 You can dig it
73 It doesn't happen again
75 "Tapestry" label
76 Verbal vote
77 ___ for tat

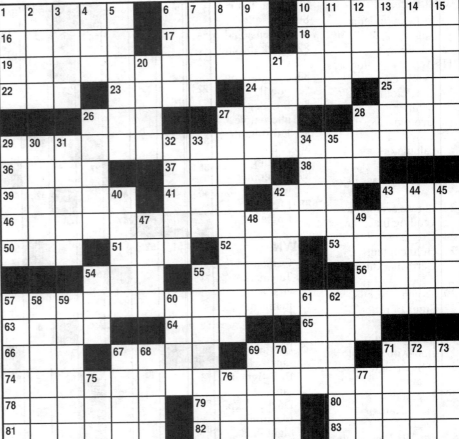

SHOP TALK   by Patrick Jordan
11 Down was a song on their 1975 album "Wish You Were Here."

ACROSS

1 Walks in the waiting room
6 Abundant amount
11 Subzero temperature sign
16 Take flight to unite
17 Book before Joel
18 Parsley family herb
19 Less experienced
20 Sorrowful statement
21 Filibuster broadcaster
22 **Quip: Part 1**
25 Terrific time
26 The Blue Angels, e.g.
30 **Quip: Part 2**
35 Coin creation process
36 Fixed-payment plan
37 Brood
38 Gun, in gangster flicks
39 "Guideposts" editor Norman Vincent
40 Inherently
42 Shuts down
43 **Quip: Part 3**
47 Ready, briefly
49 Going hungry
50 Takes way too much of
53 Dinny's master Alley
54 Excessive quantity
55 Portuguese wine
57 Emulates Elvis
59 **Quip: Part 4**
61 Inheritance tax target
62 Publisher Nast
63 **Quip: Part 5**
70 Shirtless basketball team
73 Present at birth
74 Sign off on
75 Successful job applicant
76 Leaning
77 City where Galileo taught
78 Put forward
79 Reacts to a haymaker
80 Hits a housefly

DOWN

1 Durable do
2 Jai ___
3 Part of Batman's disguise
4 Pentathlon event
5 Middle Ages menial
6 Portrayer of Irma and Tess
7 Marks in a list
8 Fielding percentage element
9 Handed out hands
10 Marquis de ___
11 Pink Floyd's "Welcome to the ___"
12 Sunday paper piece
13 Autumn chill
14 Chant at the Olympics
15 Rep.'s colleague
23 Demise notice
24 Chiang Kai-shek's capital
27 Antacid ingredient
28 "Zounds!" alternative
29 Ping-Pong partitions
30 Blasting or thinking follower
31 1969 Three Dog Night hit
32 Chaotic place
33 Cup-shaped flower
34 Security interest
35 Engage in slam-dancing, say
37 TV's eloquent equine
40 Fizzling-out sound
41 Grandmother of Enos
42 Tribal bigwig
44 Keir of "Bunny Lake is Missing"
45 It's hard to bear
46 Cryptogram's key
47 Be a model student?
48 Bingo card quintet
51 Post-meal morsel
52 Highlander's "Hardly!"
54 Makes arrangements for
55 "Tin Lizzies"
56 Impressionist
58 Not as humble
59 Kim's "The Facts of Life" role
60 Summonable by phone
62 Box from an orchard
64 Watchdog's warning
65 Mouths, in slang
66 Raptor's ripper
67 Alan in "Paper Lion"
68 Force to flee
69 "Jabberwocky" starter
70 "Steady as ___ goes!"
71 "Kid-tested, mother-approved" cereal
72 High dudgeon

90 BAD GROWING CONDITIONS by Barry C. Silk
52 Across was also a pen name of Jonathan Swift.

ACROSS

1 Otalgia
8 Balmy
12 Quantities: Abbr.
16 Red-flagged item
17 Sikkim's global area
18 City near Sparks
19 Body of water south of Orsk
20 **Start of a quote by 83 Across**
22 Rod McKuen song
23 Sadistic
25 Gene Vincent's "___ Lovin' "
26 Hams it up
29 Doesn't play
30 **More of quote**
35 Was in charge of
36 For instance
37 Texas tea
38 ___ Kan dog food
41 Trying experience
43 Fibula, e.g.
45 Narrow furrow
47 **More of quote**
50 Of the hipbone
51 "Tosca" highlight
52 Word said with a wave of the hand
53 Chicago hrs.
54 Concorde
55 Early second-century year
56 Chinese menu name
57 **More of quote**
62 Flood
65 PC key
66 Make ___ (phone)
67 Geo model
69 Va. neighbor
73 **End of quote**
75 Pizza topping
78 Away from the wind
79 Some time ago
80 Department stores
81 Pocket protector user
82 Lacking width and depth
83 **Source of quote**

DOWN

1 Mus. key with four sharps
2 Rhine tributary
3 Anti-piracy org.
4 "Never sold before!"
5 "CSI" network
6 Do ground work?
7 "Just as it should be!"
8 1960s dance
9 1968 U.S. Open winner
10 Cambodian capital
11 Ginnie ___
12 Songlike
13 Thaws
14 Fed. security
15 Some convertibles
21 Eponymous source of "Dracula"
24 Buttons in "Sayonara"
27 Byzantine wall art
28 Electric toothbrush brand
29 Sidekick
30 Line around the globe
31 Ex-British PM Macmillan
32 Breaks up
33 "Crime and Punishment" heroine
34 Appearance
38 Yamaguchi on skates
39 "Say it ___, Joe!"
40 Bora Bora enclosure
42 That, in Toledo
43 Tournament spot
44 Geisha's sash
45 Inflexible
46 Word ignored in indexes
48 Survive
49 Offer a viewpoint
54 ___ Thérèse, Quebec
55 Optimum snorkeling conditions
57 Projected
58 Tangelo trademark
59 Exchanged words?
60 "___ who?"
61 Stretching muscle
62 Six-Day War general
63 Nice school
64 Longtime "Today" host
67 Ivy in Philly
68 Kind of pudding
70 Irene of "Fame" fame
71 Opposin'
72 Did "Time"
74 "Hinky Dinky Parlay ___"
76 Ray of the Indigo Girls
77 "America's Next Top Model" network

91 SPEECH THERAPY   by Victor Fleming
Elijah rode 2 Down on the highway to heaven.

ACROSS

1 UML sublanguage
4 Early TV host
8 Peak in les Alpes
12 Zap
15 Sorority letter
16 Yokel
17 Bluff in Banff
18 Brazilian port
19 **Source of quotation (with 73-A)**
21 Envelope abbreviation
22 Pose a poser
23 Prior
24 Diddley and Derek
26 Not similar
28 Kinswoman
29 Favoring
30 Was meddlesome
31 **Start of a quotation**
36 Camp Swampy pooch
37 Rip-roaring time
38 Long fish
39 "Go on!"
40 Iams eater
41 Scarf for Mae West
42 Have a hankering
43 Sea spots
47 **Middle of quotation**
48 African menace
49 Freshmen, usually
50 "How wonderful!"
51 One of the gang
52 Ticket info
53 Mini-albums
54 Not tough at all
55 Yarn spinner
59 **End of quotation**
63 Hardly domestic
64 HMO concern
65 Protection
66 Chase scene din
68 ___ Plaines
69 House of games
70 Make advances on
71 Errand runner
73 **See 19 Across**
75 "The Wedding Banquet" director Lee
76 Drove like mad
77 Part of a pot
78 Inc. kin
79 More, in Cancún
80 Figure of Arthurian legend
81 Impoverished
82 Meth.

DOWN

1 Magic city
2 Elijah's transport
3 What Rittenhouse Square apartments aren't
4 Radio button
5 Kinswoman
6 "Alias" network
7 Pump shoes
8 New corp. hires
9 Food morsel
10 Au ___
11 Play with matches?
12 Playground "coward"
13 Exposure
14 Coupling
20 Right-hand page, in printing
25 Sch. in Tulsa
27 Apartment occupant
29 Apartment
30 "Not guilty," e.g.
32 Gets on, so to speak
33 Marquee sign
34 Boaters pull them
35 "The ___ Reader"
40 Barnum and 109
41 "Poppycock!"
42 Fashion inits.
43 "Me!"
44 Appear to be
45 Jumps over
46 Salmon, at times
47 Go for
48 El alternative
50 German automaker
51 Go by
53 Dodger's forte
54 Photographer's cover
55 Hanger-on
56 Laura ___ Wilder
57 Grapefruit juice property
58 Transmits twice
60 Like baroque architecture
61 Skater of cinema
62 Not as small
66 Did the butterfly
67 New Rochelle college
68 Owner's proof
69 Pilot leader?
72 Red Baron's Fokker ___
74 "Mrs. Lennon" singer

92 JOINT EFFORT by Norma Steinberg
56 Across can be seen in New York's Museum of Modern Art.

ACROSS

1 Put on the line
5 "With boughs of holly ___ . . ."
11 Harbor sights
16 Somalian supermodel
17 Aphrodite's beloved
18 New Zealand native
19 Incan homeland
20 Deliberately ignore
22 Gummed labels
24 Hur or Gurion
25 Exist
26 Hawk family member
27 Defeated, slangily
29 Diarist Anais
30 Electrical units
32 Actor Diesel
33 Heeds the alarm
35 Put at 000
36 Rand McNally product
37 Author Rand
38 Follow
39 Like some alliances
42 Diner sign
46 He played Zorba
47 Sleep soundly?
48 Zellweger in "Leatherheads"
49 Progeny
50 Basic pantry item
51 Ruhr Valley city
52 Mouse-sighting cry
54 "¡___ favor, amigo!"
55 Coffee package info
56 Van Gogh's "The ___ Night"
59 Farm layer
60 Embers
61 Rocky outcropping
62 "Ragged Dick" author
64 Postprandial sound
65 Iranian coin
67 To, to Hans
68 Expressway
72 "Cheers" patrons, e.g.
75 Add and delete
76 Parisian waterway
77 Placid
78 Lease subject
79 Put on, as a show
80 Romantic meetings
81 Heroic tale

DOWN

1 Pulls apart
2 "___ a Man": Ciardi
3 Punjab wrap
4 Give in
5 Sides of an issue
6 Really, really like
7 Online chuckles
8 ". . . ___ lived happily ever after"
9 Capital city on the Tajo
10 Hearth heap
11 Dallas campus
12 Corridor
13 Element called I
14 Knighted conductor André
15 Sea nymphs
21 Street sign
23 Tabby's baby
27 Rapper
28 Hudson's frequent costar
30 Locale
31 Davis in "Harry and Son"
32 Pat's cohost
34 Funny jokes
35 Demands: Abbr.
36 Has to
40 Synthetic fabric
41 Contemptuous expression
43 Adams who wrote "Born Free and Equal"
44 Adolescents
45 Gmail command
48 Converted, in a way
50 NASA success
53 Pitching stat
56 Cause of burnout
57 Latrine
58 Mecca locale
59 Playboy Mansion resident
60 "___! Foiled again!"
63 Sheraton patron
64 Charred
66 Yearn
68 Polo shirts
69 "Why, the very ___!"
70 Chess VIP
71 Blues guitarist Baker
73 Tiny
74 Help with the dishes

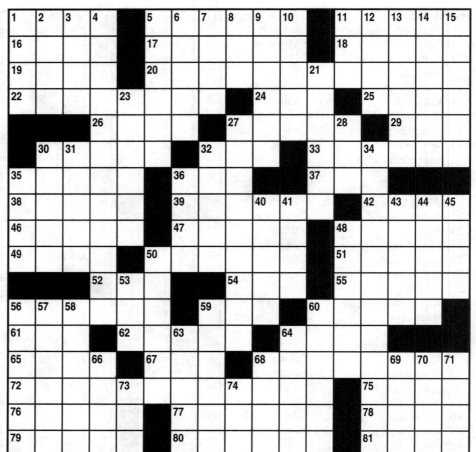

93 COMICAL CLUES by Matt Ginsberg
Joe Cocker covered 59 Across in 1970.

ACROSS

1 Pest-removal word
6 Trickle-down effect
11 ___ deux
16 Flip comment
17 Head lights
18 The end of many attorneys
19 Shake in bed
20 Study aid
21 A little night music
22 Gets a handle on
24 One who's always right
26 Add ends
27 Tried to lose
29 Have a fling
30 Lord of the ring
32 Beginning of a cure
34 Calling up trouble
37 Adam or Eve?
42 What the clueless have
43 Sicilian volcano
44 Sting
45 Violin string
46 British ram
48 Abbr. for Roget
50 Mouth opening
51 Backbreaker for a camel
54 Nair rival
56 Twisted
59 1967 Box Tops hit
61 Gets back to business
62 Route LXVI, e.g.
63 Coin
65 Start to kick
68 Tennis player who often raised a racket
70 Fork setting
74 Spinning out of control
76 Gilda "SNL" character
78 "Mission possible" group
79 Like a not-so-fine whine
81 Letter opener
82 Check some stock
83 Replace with dots
84 Mexican cigar
85 A lot of assassins
86 Orders to go
87 Guys who use come-on lines

DOWN

1 Bred winners
2 Carbon copy
3 A way with numbers
4 Helped
5 Heated competition
6 Brew that will make you wise?
7 Person in charge of liner notes?
8 Russell Crowe's middle name
9 Knight stick
10 "Oremus"
11 Kind of tense
12 When people like to pay taxes?
13 Technique for viewing some slides
14 ___ Salaam
15 Still-life subjects
23 Roundup rope
25 Compass points
28 Artist's pad
31 Sweet ending
33 Withdrawal problem
34 Fear of Frankfurters
35 River's end
36 Saltpetre
38 Part of RIT
39 Do a make-up job
40 Italian shroud city
41 Big pictures
43 Blade for Aramis
47 Like military boots?
49 Reunion attendees
52 Turn into an extraterrestrial?
53 Believer in spirits
55 Formerly, formerly
57 Louis XVI, e.g.
58 Made the cut
60 Work behind bars
61 Fixes a clog
64 High-stepping occasion
65 Union member
66 Whits
67 Slip cover
69 Gamut
71 First ding in the morning
72 "What's in ___?"
73 Exorcist's concern
75 "The Secret Storm" family
77 "¿Cómo ___?"
80 Start of a pleasing expression

94

"SHAPE UP!" by Arlan and Linda Bushman
Orodruin is another name for Mount Doom (see 39 Across).

ACROSS

1 Marine prowlers
5 Hitchcock gem?
10 Fissures
16 Three Rivers river
17 Speculate
18 Superficial
19 Ready-made response
21 On the go
22 Ultimatum
23 Like much testimony
25 "Casablanca" croupier
26 Tread softly
28 Give way
29 Lively dance
30 Voyager's FTL velocity
36 Strike out
38 "Swan Lake" swan
39 Traveler to Mount Doom
41 Lab cultures
45 Utter a harsh cry
46 Waive
47 Hooded jacket
48 Puppeteer Baird
49 Penicillin source
51 "The Bourne Identity" org.
52 Throw
54 Sully
55 Kind of iron
56 Mariner's friend in "Waterworld"
57 "Rooster Cogburn" star
58 Beatles vamp
59 River of Aragon
61 Home of the Fighting Irish
63 Zenith
66 Man from Moo
68 Old hand
69 Drawn
70 Black suit
73 Musketeer of fiction
78 On the line
80 Martini adornment
82 Dorm cohort
83 Impassive
84 Hollywood's Raines
85 Bug
86 Links coup
87 Some browsers

DOWN

1 Not in condition
2 "This could be bad!"
3 Whirring sound
4 Handful
5 Hoofer's move
6 Not participate, with "out"
7 Quarries
8 From the top
9 Ciphers
10 Morph
11 Ad ___
12 Hyde, to Jekyll
13 Muck
14 "Seven" or "10"
15 Peachy
20 Blunder
24 Swiss watch name
27 "Robinson Crusoe" author
30 Rock
31 Brody in "The Pianist"
32 Venetian bridge
33 Layer
34 Corrections list
35 Summer doldrums
37 Set down
40 Piece with pips
42 Roofed passageway
43 Wrinkled morsel
44 Glided along
46 Small ___
47 PC keyboard tag
49 Spill the beans
50 A point ahead
53 Employee scheduling perk
55 Semi section
57 Moth's temptation
58 Abbreviated
60 Rise rapidly
62 Stupor
63 Video game pioneer
64 "Cry, the Beloved Country" author
65 Guilder replacements
67 Throb
71 Gamma preceder
72 Skyline obscurer
74 Thunderstruck
75 Eight furlongs
76 Vacation spot
77 Sheriff's badge
79 Oft-bracketed word
81 Shale extract

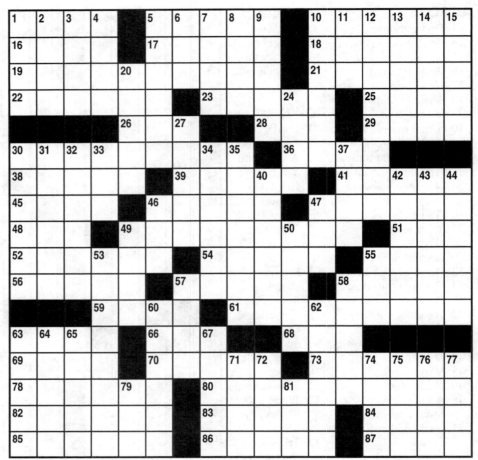

95 BOOB TUBE by Lisa Damiano
The title is appropriate for the quip below.

ACROSS

1 Andy Warhol's genre
7 Gogol's "___ Bulba"
12 Afrikaner
16 Put topsoil on
17 As a friend, to Michele
18 Women's magazine
19 One-cellers
20 Spring sound
21 Bank guarantor: Abbr.
22 ___ facto
23 "Biography" network
24 "The Prince of ___" (1991)
25 **Start of a quip**
28 Darkness prefix
30 TV horse
31 Subatomic particle
32 Members of AMA
35 **Part 2 of quip**
41 "Don Carlos" princess
42 Prefix meaning 100
43 "River has ___; Mississippi has four"
44 "Hallelujah, I'm ___" (folk song)
45 **Part 3 of quip**
48 Resolution
49 The scarlet letter
50 Cockney's distinction
51 Start of a Neapolitan song
52 **Part 4 of quip**
57 Cookbook abbr.
58 Chevy pickup
59 No, in Hilo
60 Relief giver
62 **End of quip**
67 Mandalay Bay VIP
69 Bootlicker
72 Eternally

73 Devon in "2 Fast 2 Furious"
74 "Divina Commedia" author
75 Get rid of potholes
77 Slow migration
78 Pass in the Sinai
79 Amatory
80 Container weight
81 Blacksmith's block
82 Purpose

DOWN

1 Braid
2 What Marilyn Monroe had
3 Bel ___ cheese
4 New Jersey's Perth or South
5 Blakey of CNN
6 Dolphin stats
7 Diva Renata
8 At another time
9 Police action
10 Jason Bourne et al.
11 Composer Romberg
12 Be appropriate to
13 Virginia's nickname
14 Nobelist Wiesel
15 45s and 78s: Abbr.
23 Pub offerings
24 Musical sound
26 CCCII x III
27 Paul's role in "Exodus"
29 French nobleman
31 Michelin tire
33 Mano a mano code
34 Pot winner, e.g.

35 "___ Up" (Queen song)
36 Brooklyn Dodgers field
37 Stereo system component
38 Mischa the violinist
39 Midwest hub
40 Use a divining rod
45 Cabaret
46 Throw a party
47 McCarthy aide Roy
51 City on the Oka
53 Start of North Carolina's motto
54 Short end of the stick
55 Like caviar

56 Whole shebang
61 Two peas in a pod
63 Greyhound station
64 Egg-shaped
65 "Mighty Lak' a Rose" composer
66 Straight up and down
67 Power unit
68 Dance at a bar mitzvah
70 Where "Lost" is found
71 "Volsunga Saga" king
74 Conductor's deg.
75 Potuguese king
76 Shore bird

96 BEDROOM SCENES   by Patrick Jordan
. . . and these scenes are all rated G!

ACROSS

1 Pursuer of the Penguin
7 Pop in on
12 ___ regia (gold dissolver)
16 Finish a respiration
17 Fable's moral, often
18 Sound from Barney on "The Simpsons"
19 Crystal-lined stones
20 Arcade coin
21 Wildly popular fad
22 Punta del ___
24 Fairy tale with a bedroom scene (with 40-A)
26 Avila abode
29 "Attack!," to a guard dog
31 "Rumor has it . . ."
32 Appetizing smell
34 Acquaintance of Estragon
37 Comment to the playgoers
40 See 24 Across
42 Puts on the record
43 Linus's constant companion
44 Oman money
46 They used to spin LPs
47 Fairy tale with a bedroom scene (with 72-A)
51 Join a quilting bee
54 Vice squad concern
55 Metrical unit
59 Oft-coiffed dog
62 Fairy tale with a bedroom scene
64 Hawk's home
65 Contentious matter
66 Mall or mine follower
67 Absorb academically
69 0° longitude hrs.
71 Budgetary reductions
72 See 47 Across
76 "Uh-huh"

78 1/6 inch, to a printer
79 Takes in
81 Disreputable
85 Rooster's weapon
86 ___-Lay (35-D company)
87 More frilly
88 Set eyes on
89 Silver or Scout, say
90 Joints under spats

DOWN

1 Request with clasped hands
2 Fireman's chopper
3 Even if, to a bard
4 Was extremely profitable
5 Pints poured in pubs
6 Pest-control targets
7 Tannery vessel
8 Role model
9 "The Interlopers" author
10 "No need to explain the punchline"
11 Virginia, in statehood rank
12 Shoulder-to-shoulder
13 Dug out, as marble
14 Light a fire under
15 Did a spoof of
23 When prime time starts in NYC
25 Be recumbent
26 Fuel injector's predecessor, briefly
27 Seed covering
28 Spritzer ingredient
30 Romantic murmur
33 Hieroglyphic cross

35 Corn-chip brand
36 God whose throne is named Hlidskjalf
38 Four-time NBA MVP
39 Sidewinder's shape
41 They're a-laying in song
42 1985 John Malkovich film
45 Private high school
48 Tawdry toupees
49 "Do the Right Thing" pizzeria
50 Random sampling
51 Hydropathic treatment site
52 Help-wanted ad abbr.
53 Soccer event since 1930
56 Creamy color

57 Burlesque bit
58 Recipe amts.
60 Regimen-related
61 Judah's mother
63 Clumsy fellow
65 Not entirely
68 Navigation hazards
70 Electricity pioneer Nikola
72 Cathedral area
73 Jack Frost's assaults
74 Canal opened in 1825
75 Pre-deal payment
77 Country crooner Jackson
80 Lawn patch
82 Have an affliction
83 Suez terminus?
84 Soph and sr., e.g.

97 WIDE-OPEN SPACES   by Frank Longo
An 80-word themeless challenger.

ACROSS

1 A user may burn one
13 Wonka portrayer
17 String quartet instruments
18 Profess
19 Mutual influences
20 Coquettish trick
21 Words of concurrence
22 Je ne ___ quoi
23 Stuff in a pencil
24 Puerto Rico's chief port
25 Garmin's navigation
28 Cole ___ (fashion label)
29 Scribe
30 Mandrake the Magician's sidekick
32 Home to Central Michigan U.
36 Take ___ (go sightseeing)
37 "Bye-bye!"
38 It used to streak in the sky
39 Dept. concerned with cleaning up
40 Tree knots
41 Napoli night
43 Apt to artifice
44 Wait longer than
45 ". . . has ___ and hungry look": Shak.
46 Deejay of top 40 countdowns
49 Cranks up
50 Editorializes
51 Timewalker of Valiant Comics
53 Bishop's bailiwick
54 Car parker
55 "My Big Fat Greek Wedding" star
59 I, O or U, but not A or E: Abbr.
60 Forestry
64 She ranks in Raipur
65 Opposite of patriotic
66 "Behold!," at the Forum
67 Connector of many calls
68 Wedded trio?
69 Warbling women

DOWN

1 Year in Trajan's reign
2 Vietnam's Ngo ___ Diem
3 Ecclesiastical court of appeal in Rome
4 Professeur's charge
5 "Never Surrender" singer
6 Rampaging
7 Maker of Nehi
8 Holdups
9 Put right
10 Old comic actor Eric
11 Company eschewer
12 "Sum" is a form of it
13 TV's "___ Creek"
14 Annual LPGA Tour event in France
15 Land of Opportunity neighbor
16 Some action words are in it
24 Potpie bit
25 Like hotbeds
26 Chief residence of the Dalai Lama until 1959
27 Expressionless, hushed state, as from being stunned
29 Little, in Limoges
31 Chinese emperor ___ Tsung
33 Razz
34 Cytosine, thymine, and uracil
35 Going down the wrong road, perhaps
37 Gull-like bird
41 Needle stone
42 Boff ending
44 Lets go through
47 Bond and No, e.g.
48 In the time left
49 Base greeter?
52 Like some lots and stares
55 ___ verde (Portuguese wine)
56 St. Louis suburb
57 Camper's activity, informally
58 Puts securely away
60 Cheeseheads
61 Spanish indefinite article
62 Few and far between
63 Club with lodges

UTTER NONSENSE   by Jay Sullivan
Hustlers should know the answer to 43 Across.

ACROSS

1 Sweet thing
6 The end of ___
11 Downs town
16 "Norma" or "Martha"
17 Peace proponents
18 Figure of speech
19 "Beyond the Sea" subject (2004)
20 Nullifies
21 Biblical prophet
22 Yodel?
25 Substitute for
26 Something Sajak sells
27 Not working
32 In custody
37 Typically
38 Ski boost
39 King or queen
40 Rapid Ryan
41 Playground retort
43 Blue-striped pool ball
44 Cuss?
48 Casting choice
49 Small praise
50 Becker of "L.A. Law"
52 Sacred Egyptian bull
54 Welcome sights
55 More voluble
57 Dated
59 Symbol of witchcraft
60 Racer blade
61 Ladies' men
63 "Oops!"?
71 Roulette bet
72 They're related
73 Southfork family
75 One who takes potshots
76 Act badly
77 "It's true"
78 Backboard, familiarly
79 Intuit
80 Join forces

DOWN

1 Coal porter
2 October birthstone
3 Famed fiddler
4 Apt name for a colleen
5 Yahoo honcho
6 Dutch uncle's nephew?
7 Ready for hanging
8 Lloyd Webber title character
9 Over-exposed, in a way
10 NRA or NCAA
11 Anesthetic gas
12 Way of getting things done
13 1998 National League MVP
14 Autobahn auto
15 It's what's for dinner
23 Unable to cut it
24 Dip stick?
27 Dapper fellow
28 Atomic alternative
29 Crusaders' foe
30 Shrinking sea
31 Scam
33 Test group
34 1998 Oscar winner
35 Biblical prophet
36 Home room
38 Sets straight
41 Even so
42 Prayerful figure
45 Think well of
46 Sound of music
47 Mother of the Valkyries
48 Rarer than rare
51 Afore of yore
53 Larry, Curly, and Moe
55 "Time will tell"
56 MIT or VMI
58 Is undecided
59 Forensic evidence
62 Green border
63 Rugged rock
64 Make a stir
65 Colorado town
66 Deli inventory
67 What's cooking
68 Lottery exclamation
69 Taylor of "Six Feet Under"
70 Put in stitches
74 "I'm impressed"

99 RENOWN PHRASE by Patrick Jordan

The original name of 21 Across was Truman Streckfus Persons.

ACROSS

1 Galileo Galilei Airport site
5 Denver boot, for one
10 In force
15 Tweak text
16 Mansion's counterpart
17 At peace
18 Simeon's mother
19 Ancient Athens marketplace
20 "M*A*S*H" procedure
21 **Truman Capote quip: Part 1**
24 They're filled with bills
25 Tango maneuver
26 Canonized mlle.
27 With intervening space
30 "Gets down" at a disco
34 Rorschach or road follower
35 **Quip: Part 2**
40 Alts.
41 Mashes a mosquito
42 Celebrated shortstop Pee Wee
43 English Lit assignments
45 Science of motion forces
48 Hunter on high
49 Snobbish sort
50 Vaudeville legend Eddie
51 **Quip: Part 3**
55 "What ___ you thinking?"
56 Costing a dime
57 Supermarket fleet
58 Hearth particle
61 Store receipt word
62 Quatrain composer
64 **End of quip**
72 Kind of couplet
73 Mountain bike options
74 Skin cream additive
75 Fixes upright
76 Water or rust, chemically
77 Made a present of
78 Office array
79 Parachute fabric
80 Set one's sights on

DOWN

1 Money, in slang
2 Skull session result
3 "The King and I" backdrop
4 In essence
5 Yawning pit
6 Corporate symbols
7 Anthony Eden's earldom
8 European blackbird
9 Modeling material for kids
10 ___ Beach, FL
11 Desert description
12 Reads (through)
13 Foundry bar
14 Plow innovator John
17 Visit briefly
22 Unintelligible Addams
23 1958's Best Picture
27 For each
28 Czar known as "the Great"
29 Tear into
30 "All ___ are off!" ("No guarantees!")
31 Game extensions, briefly
32 Long-necked frog eater
33 "Ignore the dele"
35 Fall heir to
36 Imitate a shrew
37 Dairy youngster
38 Chaperone, e.g.
39 Enthusiastic agreement
41 As of
44 Simpleton
45 Sailing speed unit
46 Short notice?
47 Fish-fowl connector
49 "Together" prefix
52 Monkeyshines
53 Decode a bar code
54 Shape in a honeycomb
55 Light bulb number
57 Animation studio sheet
58 Throbbed
59 ___ Khan (Kipling tiger)
60 Start of Ed's late-night intro
62 Veteran TV announcer Don
63 Gridiron retiree Merlin
65 Prepare to fire
66 Hobbyists' buys
67 Cheesecake adjective?
68 Pony Express delivery
69 Oil of ___
70 Crafted burlap
71 Cry out for

100   TURNING POINTS   by Elizabeth C. Gorski
The embedded title can be found at 43 Across.

ACROSS

1 Neat as ___
5 Athlete who's very goal-oriented?
12 Cut from the same cloth
16 An ex of Burt
17 Fleece producers
18 Marco's "well"
19 Patient wear*
21 QED middle
22 Hitching posts?
23 Hemingway's "In ___ Time"
24 They're developed by Mr. Universe
25 Future docs' exams
26 1960s pop song by the Winstons*
30 Veggie burger's base
31 Agcy. once led by Leon Panetta
32 CPR experts
33 Queen of Thebes, in mythology
34 Pull back
37 Ltr. holders
39 "___ Rebel": Crystals
40 Per se
41 Surveyor's measure
42 Thin cookie
43 TITLE
46 "Rush, Rush" singer
49 Reverse
50 "Law & Order" actor Farina
54 Places with going rates?
55 Foil's cousin
56 Bridge expert
57 Compass user's suffix
58 Comedienne Charlotte
59 Dart game locale
60 Stanley, for one
61 Bit of nasty gossip*
65 Caterpillar's rival
67 Assn. of lodges
68 Singer DiFranco
69 "Brady Bunch," e.g.
70 Claude of champagne fame
71 One-time ABC police drama*
74 "... ___ take this charm from off her sight": Shak.
75 Got by
76 Barbra's "Funny Girl" costar
77 Stop dreaming?
78 Legendary king of Athens
79 Eye piece

DOWN

1 Granada landmark
2 Sticks in a game room
3 Split seconds
4 Try to bite, as one's heels
5 Yoga class needs
6 Dock workers' gp.
7 Composure
8 Home of Queen Beatrix (with "The")
9 Tough nut to crack
10 Gaping mouth
11 ISP choice
12 Red as ___ (embarrassed)
13 Babushka
14 Sort of
15 Common URL ending
20 Agcy. with many agents
24 Opp. of negative
26 Small quantity?
27 Original ELO member
28 Hosp. units
29 Loud laugh
31 Koko Head island
35 "Tell Me Something Good" band
36 Earth Hour subj.
37 Slowly destroy
38 Grammy winner Peter
39 Blue Rodeo's "___ Hit Me Yet"
41 Prom-night nightmare?
42 House bird
44 Indian coin
45 River of Germany
46 Guinness of "Star Wars"
47 Island of French Polynesia
48 Warning on a Christmas present
51 Happy hour?
52 "You bet!"
53 Vatican City basilica
55 Shucker's spike
56 Pierre, S. ___
58 It may be toast
59 Way out of Manhattan
62 Funny Fields
63 The Pine Tree State
64 Karenina and namesakes
65 Tony winner McAnuff
66 Praise
69 Foam
70 Small gull
71 NYC subway line
72 "Well, ___-di-dah"
73 ___ d'esprit (witty comment)

101 "HUMOR ME!" by Robert A. Doll

22 Across has a champagne, cigar, and tank named after him.

ACROSS

1 Hardens
7 Any day now
11 Comment to the audience
16 Be a buttinsky
17 Miler's concern
18 Puts on cargo
19 Melodious
20 Emulate Chagall
21 "Three Billy Goats Gruff" baddie
22 **Speaker of quote**
25 ___ Anne de Beaupré
26 Purple shade
27 Parts of a min.
31 Ethnic cuisine
34 Nextel Cup org.
39 **Quote: Part 1**
43 Like Silver's rider
44 In ___ res
45 Flat-topped rise
46 Predispositions
47 Bleep out
49 More than twice
51 Time on the job
52 Move like molasses
56 Beaver State city
58 Blue-ribbon
59 **Quote: Part 2**
61 Kind of union
63 Long, long time
64 Just for men
65 Slammer unit
67 Literary monogram
70 Win at "Last Comic Standing"?
79 Antilles native
80 "Triple" ice jump
81 Snarl
82 Endangered perissodactyl
83 Untouched?
84 Branch of the deer family?
85 Forefinger
86 See 2 Down
87 Pine products

DOWN

1 "Heartbreak House" playwright
2 "Real Men" singer (with 86-A)
3 "___ go bragh!"
4 1961 space chimp
5 Leans, at sea
6 High-hatter
7 Design detail
8 Four-letter word
9 Takes up space
10 Jawaharlal
11 Tennis great Gibson
12 Madras dress
13 Hollywood favorite
14 Apple rival
15 Immigrant's class: Abbr.
23 New Jersey cagers
24 Manhattan sch.
27 Drucker of "Green Acres"
28 Jet seat
29 Tylenol #3 ingredient
30 Fair-___ beauty
32 Limelight lover
33 Forum greeting
35 Horse-drawn vehicles
36 Amour-propre
37 Rabbit ears
38 Court matter
40 "Big" Syracuse conference
41 Equal: Comb. form
42 Dirty dog
46 Fabergé cologne
48 Beluga yield
50 "For ___ a jolly . . ."
51 Cul-de-___
53 Graduate school challenge
54 Sharp turn
55 Help-wanted abbr.
57 Curate's ___
59 Editor's mark
60 Brings into play
62 Early refrigerator
66 Himalayan capital
68 Rose oil
69 Spruce Goose, e.g.
70 Chemistry Nobelist Otto
71 Like the Kalahari
72 Tarzan's transport
73 Late-night name
74 Pub potables
75 Pangolin's meal
76 Wrinkly fruit
77 Secluded valley
78 Half a matched set
79 Dernier ___ (the latest thing)

102 DROPPING ACID by Richard Silvestri
Listen to "Lucy in the Sky With Diamonds" while solving this one.

ACROSS

1 Tracking device
6 Do Little work
9 Red-white-and-blue monogram
12 "___ Didn't Care"
15 In solitary
16 Snitch
17 Cuban capitalist?
19 Close observation of commotion?
21 Moved like a dragonfly
22 Musically jarring
23 Asian holiday
25 Big name in farm equipment
26 Offshore structure
28 Abadan coin
31 Speak with forked tongue
32 Traffic snarler
37 Like the surface of the moon
40 Shark's offer
41 Mrs. Helmer
43 Candidate's concern
44 Troubles
45 Sweater size
47 Established as fact
50 Tour de France vehicles
52 Glyceride
54 On ___ (carousing)
55 Genetic
57 Port in a storm
59 "Bus Stop" playwright
60 Muscat inhabitant
62 Heat, e.g.
63 Begins litigation
64 Couric's workplace
67 Some chickens
69 Every last bit
70 Social rebuff
72 AEC successor
73 Good, in Guatemala
76 Prospector's aid
78 Rope for a trail boss
83 Kook
86 Infantile Dickens novel?
88 Crew competition

89 Blow away
90 Grace
91 Compass dir.
92 Radical '60s gp.
93 The acid dropped in this puzzle
94 Bartok and Fleck

DOWN

1 ___-tat-tat
2 Piles
3 Didus ineptus
4 Ere long
5 Word on a wanted poster
6 It may be abstract
7 War ender
8 Old number?
9 TV band
10 Mule of song
11 Gung-ho
12 Chip money?
13 "The ___ Queene": Spenser
14 By all means
18 Had a bite
20 UFO crew
24 Initial X, perhaps
27 Folklore dwarf
29 Uris hero
30 Aladdin's discovery
32 Legal out
33 General Powell
34 Result of a Berkeley degree?
35 Trouser junctures
36 Compactor input
38 The O'Hara place
39 Vanity case?
42 Sacrifice spot
46 Burton of "Star Trek: TNG"
48 Champing at the bit
49 Go formal
51 Top player
53 Scouting work
56 Sonny Shroyer role

58 Not quite
61 Chemists get a charge out of it
64 Pyle player
65 Gives the slip to
66 The word, at times
68 Deified beetle
71 Elephant of kiddie lit
74 Tony Parker's org.
75 Feedbag filler
77 Lowly member of the board?
79 Insulting
80 Fan's favorite
81 Taj Mahal site
82 Till section
84 Old Ford model
85 Vegas opening
87 Emmy winner Arthur

NINE-PIN REALITY by Victor Fleming
"The Peter Principle" author on everyday existence.

ACROSS

1 Key letter
5 Mr. Woodley of "Blondie"
9 Allan Sherman camp
16 Came to rest
17 Skin-care brand
18 Put in a crate
19 NFL Hall-of-Famer Ronnie
20 "The Plot Against America" author
21 Ariel, for one
22 **Laurence Peter quotation: Part I**
25 Some time ago
26 Not with
27 Shoshonean
30 African cape name
32 **Quotation: Part II**
36 Boss's Day mo.
37 Slow start
39 "Apostolados" artist
40 Tikrit's land
42 Sevilla now
46 Get prone
47 1984 Peace Nobelist
48 **Quotation: Part III**
50 Fill to the gills
54 When Dijon gets hot
56 Bergen-born, say
57 Bygone pol. units
58 Firm
62 Sushi bar order
64 Fields persona
65 **Quotation: Part IV**
69 Like some pain
71 Prefix for center
72 Presently
73 Operation memento
74 **Quotation: Part V**
81 Sidelong pass
83 1962 Ursula Andress film
84 Winter forecast
85 Piram or Eschol
86 Toaster brand
87 Result of overexercise
88 Badenov and Godunov
89 Godunov's no
90 Marsh growth

DOWN

1 Bouncer?
2 Morlocks' victims
3 Payment in kind
4 Come to
5 Flicka or Silver
6 North Carolina university
7 Wicker material
8 Manually
9 Resembling an emerald, say
10 Sen. Chuck Hagel follower?
11 Plot element?
12 Specify
13 Generally
14 "Agnus ___"
15 Subjoin
23 Frozen beverage brand
24 Capt.'s underlings
28 Private eye
29 That, to Juan
30 Sports equipment manufacturer
31 Stockings shade
32 #1 tennis player of 1975
33 "Let me think about it"
34 ___ Friday's
35 Head lock
38 Mariners' ___ Field
41 Leeds line
43 Have control of
44 Kanga's kid
45 Land south of the Medit.
49 Like many eBay items
51 Word
52 Home-run gait
53 Town in the Euganean Hills
55 Rubble-maker
58 Filly, but not a billy
59 Something to draw from
60 Earhart, e.g.
61 Gives 100%
63 Delicate, as fabric
66 Barracks bed
67 Caulfield of fiction
68 Oomph
70 Rubicon crosser
73 Schnozz
75 Pak of the LPGA
76 Kristofferson in "Millennium"
77 "I can't believe ___ the whole . . ."
78 Pulitzer playwright
79 Architect Mies van der ___
80 Scand. tongue
81 Area of experimentation
82 Te-___ cigars

104 ADAPTION SEQUEL by Bonnie L. Gentry
"Hooray for Hollywood!"

ACROSS

1 Assigned jobs
6 Flockhart role
12 Pullman, for one
15 Slippery as ___
16 Unsound
17 Dance for a luau
18 **Part I of a quip**
20 Opposite of nope
21 Intend on
22 Scholarship allowance
24 "___ make a long story short . . ."
25 Castle's protection
27 Tests without pencils
31 **Part II of quip**
36 Dark times, in literature
37 What children shouldn't touch in the kitchen
38 Sex researcher Hite
41 Frere's sister
43 She played Carmela
44 Dallas hoopster
45 **Part III of quip**
49 Monument's age: Abbr.
50 Captain in "Moby Dick"
52 Cézanne contemporary
53 Does a laundry chore
55 Extremists
57 Roseanne's first last name
59 **Part IV of quip**
64 Ranee's wrap
65 "Othello" heavy
66 Small business course?
68 Music shop fixtures
72 Cognitive
74 Do some tub-thumping
77 **Part V of quip**
79 Thumbs-up voters
80 Ecological systems
81 Tastiness
82 More than miffed
83 Bull Run general Jeb
84 Fake handle

DOWN

1 Forces down
2 Having hands, clockwise
3 Ratifying body
4 One with an address
5 Shutter part
6 Degree from Parsons, perhaps
7 Implying an origin
8 Fit up against
9 Appropriate for kids K–12
10 Mounted on
11 U-shaped musical instrument
12 Signal to enter
13 Menu attribution words
14 Pep rally word
17 Moisturize
19 "Time and tide wait for ___ "
23 Negative links
26 Photo ___ (PR occasions)
28 Like one end of a battery terminal
29 Assessed, as a tax
30 Dieter's bane
32 Caught sight of
33 Thomas Crown caper
34 Deck suit complement
35 Other, in Oaxaca
38 "Street" intelligence
39 "Oh, yeah, that's funny"
40 Escapee, at times
41 Hearing or sight, e.g.
42 Tijuana yell
46 He played Yuri in "Doctor Zhivago"
47 Lowland, poetically
48 Factory owners: Abbr.
51 Cuts evenly
54 Monopoly avenue
56 Kept in the loop, briefly
57 Seek financial aid?
58 Subject for a wine connoisseur
60 Jack's Soviet counterpart
61 Poughkeepsie college
62 Army creatures?
63 Gauguin's Tahitian autobiography
67 Cards and Bucs
69 Does a bank job
70 Pitch ___ (react angrily)
71 ___ En-lai
73 She, in Venice
74 33 or 45, e.g.
75 Parseghian of Notre Dame
76 Shoemate of Wynken and Blynken
78 "Saving Private Ryan" craft, for short

ACROSS

1 Harry Potter's rival
6 Dance studio support
11 Stage name of Tracy Marrow
15 Lindsay Lohan hit
17 Natural soothers
18 It was lost for want of a nail
19 Australian penguin
20 Number for nine?
21 Judge's seat
22 Christina Claire Ciminella
24 Snack from a kosher deli
25 Barrel rider's venue
26 German article
28 Indy 500 entrant
31 Reginald Dwight
36 "Cuchi-Cuchi" girl
37 Spec attachment
39 Shortly
40 Deadly viper
41 Nellie for whom a toast was named
43 Appear to be
44 Declan Patrick McManus
48 Board haphazardly
50 Weaker alternative to a pen?
51 Some upperclassmen: Abbr.
54 Tiny points of land
55 "See ___ care"
56 Gordon Sumner
58 Yvette Marie Stevens
61 Watches closely
63 City on the Rhone
64 "Love & Pride" singer Davis
65 Reference book
69 Geraldine Halliwell
74 Agitate
75 Hindu principle
76 Highest
77 Big fusses
78 Actress-director Keaton
79 Boxer's sequence
80 Paul Hewson
81 Apollo's birthplace
82 Yucky

DOWN

1 Attract
2 Giuliani of politics
3 "You got that right!"
4 Hair stylist, at times
5 Venezuelan river
6 Bluegrass instrument
7 MLB family name
8 14-line verse
9 Alter again
10 Fig. from a mechanic
11 Novel ID
12 Milky spiced tea
13 Ages and ages
14 One kind of support
16 ___ message
23 Mountaintop homes
24 Doghouse
27 ___ about (gossiped)
28 Color TV pioneer
29 Sighs of relief
30 Alpha star in Auriga
31 Intrude
32 Hebrew heroine who dispatched Sisera
33 Assimilation process
34 Rams and bulls, e.g.
35 53-D, for one
38 Group of Oct. ballgames
41 "The Turing Option" coauthor
42 Dating from
45 Symbol of Wales
46 Essential organs
47 Three-bagger
48 Photo, for short
49 "Sort of" suffix
52 Single-helix molecule
53 Cpl.'s superior
56 Picking up
57 Frontier trading post figure
59 Immobilize
60 "The Muppet Show" drummer
62 ___ the ground
64 "The Eve of St. ___": Keats
65 Yemeni or Saudi
66 Heading on an errand list
67 Pride member
68 In addition
70 Tiny prefix
71 "Leave ___ Beaver"
72 Milk dispensers
73 Heroic verse
75 Build on

FUNNY MEN   by Ray Hamel

68 Across is the only month that can start and end on the same day.

ACROSS

1 Serves perfectly
5 Puffed-up dessert
12 Cowgirl's footwear
16 Tennis score
17 Dress
18 Problem to face?
19 Form of therapy
21 Visible
22 Like Wikipedia
23 Crossword sign
24 Voice above a tenor
25 Contractor's fig.
26 Everly Brothers hit
30 Tailor's line
32 Ship to Colchis
33 Chemist Hahn, et al.
34 Computer insert
40 Pep rally intangible
41 Not at home
42 Gremlins and Pacers
46 Like some angels
49 Runoff source
51 K–4
52 Thom in shoes
54 "But will it play in ___?"
55 May Day disaster of 1886
58 Hurriedly
62 Word after paper or razor
63 "The Wasteland" monogram
64 Showing concern
68 Short mo.
70 Richie Rich's collar
71 Court grp.
72 Live wire, so to speak
75 Make ___ (get along)
76 "Sisters" star
80 Hold, as an opinion
81 Pop singer Gloria
82 They're found under layers
83 Sleuthing canine
84 Space shuttle manuever
85 Kind of job

DOWN

1 Pet food brand
2 Ethanol source
3 Russia, to Reagan
4 Round following the quarters
5 Inventory-reduction effort
6 Special ___
7 Lines at the checkout scanner?
8 Quite a ways
9 Just caught
10 Denis of "Rescue Me"
11 "___ World" ("Sesame Street" segment)
12 Extrusive volcanic rock
13 Spotted cat
14 Ring combination
15 Joins, as with a mortise
20 Ergate
26 ___ de coeur
27 Back then
28 Secret society
29 Atlantic food fish
30 "The Glass Bead Game" author Hermann
31 Drive out by force
32 Breathing woe
35 Composer Khachaturian
36 Flask hit
37 Base VIP's
38 Dancer Miller
39 Get back into business
42 Pablo's passion
43 Scout's honor
44 Madison Avenue awards
45 Announce
47 In need of salt
48 Rotating disk
50 Saturate
53 Partnership for Peace org.
55 Coop resident
56 Letter that follows pi
57 Caboodle's partner
58 Underlying plan
59 Has compassion for
60 Cousin of the snipe
61 Field of stars?
65 Nintendo enthusiast
66 Belittle
67 1877 Twain collaborator
68 "Read this"
69 Ceased to be
72 Fashionable initials
73 RAM units
74 Ural River city
77 DDE's rank
78 More than now and then
79 Bluejacket

POTPOURRI by Barry C. Silk

47 Across was also known as Connie Mack Stadium for many years.

ACROSS

1 ___-faire
8 How many walk along the beach
16 Sweated
18 Amendment construing judicial powers
19 Eggs are a rich source for it
20 Skipper's opposite
21 Jennifer Lopez film
22 Noted exile
23 Chicago sights
24 Massage
25 Charlemagne's domain: Abbr.
26 First year of Cornelius' papacy
27 Photographer's diaphragm
30 Catch, run, and throw
32 Mackerel sharks
33 Ailurophobe's dread
34 Multichannel system
36 Madison's st.
37 Costco alternative
38 Is in the past?
39 Constantinople's empire
43 Concern
46 Fused together
47 Phillies' old home
49 Ringside shout
50 Apple core?
51 "Welcome" sights
52 Erupt
54 Varnish base
55 Draft picks
57 Einstein Bros. product
58 1958 World Cup phenom
59 Trying people: Abbr.
60 Partner of games
61 Breezily informative
64 Eastern principle
65 Org. searching for signals from space
66 More aloof
70 San Francisco Bay lighthouse
72 Feeding tubes
73 Gone with the wind
74 Tyrannical
75 Skeptical type
76 Reserve

DOWN

1 Soap containing pumice
2 Opposed to, in oaters
3 Trace amount
4 Bites
5 "American Idol" judge Cowell
6 Site reading?
7 Zoroastrian scriptures
8 "Wouldn't It Be Nice" group
9 Sacrificial settings
10 Tighten, maybe
11 Square
12 Waterlogged lowland
13 Where a weighted bat is swung
14 1887 La Scala premiere
15 Master piece?
17 Less stimulating
26 Beehive division
27 SALT subjects
28 Indian chief
29 1959 hit for Paul Anka
31 Definitely no Yankee fan
32 Had a problem with
34 Pinata filling
35 Diamond covers
36 When repeated, a Western city
40 Some are "telephoto"
41 Katmandu locale
42 Bring out
44 They give people lifts
45 Day planner, e.g.
48 It keeps your powder dry
53 Got tight
55 Historic 1942 surrender site
56 Catchall abbr.
57 Zippo fuel
58 Dragon killed by Apollo at Delphi
60 Washington State conveyance
62 Rushing sound: Var.
63 Mawkish
65 Greek portico
67 "Must have been something ___"
68 Protection
69 Flair and Ocasek
71 Exercise target

FLIPPING THE THREE-TOED SLOTH by Victor Fleming
This one wins the most original title award!

ACROSS

1 Clerical apparel
5 Sunbow producers
10 Monopoly maker
16 Tipper, for one
17 "Go ahead with your question"
18 Toyota model
19 Hansen, if married to Frankie?
21 Taste
22 Red Sea Republic
23 Country rtes.
25 They may be black or red
26 Drift
27 Après-ski drink
30 Civic club president, often
31 Rare blood type
33 Corrupt pitcher Luis?
35 Battle of ___ (1st Allied victory of WW1)
37 Helen Reddy hit
39 Queen Noor's predecessor
41 Roger Rabbit and Porky Pig
42 "Okay by me"
47 Wall images
49 Quiet
50 Filmdom's Nastassja
51 Hopping arcade character
54 Stop following?
55 Credit card charge
58 Myrna in "The Thin Man"
59 Journal of milking activity?
63 Butts
65 Feminine ends
66 Shampoo directive
68 Ankles
71 Paving block
72 Ricky, to Harriet
73 Primes
75 Clarifier's words
77 Pathway used as a test?
80 Word after yes or no
81 Keep an ___ the ground

82 Chase of "Now, Voyager"
83 Two-seater
84 Patrol mission
85 RAF awards

DOWN

1 Shoelace end
2 Noted wine valley
3 Bonk De Palma on the head?
4 Relayed
5 Guy
6 Father of famous twins
7 Go downhill fast?
8 Badge material
9 Baseball no-nos
10 Accidents
11 Marchetta in "Material Girls"
12 A hero may have it
13 "Una Paloma ___" (1975 hit song)
14 Bad
15 Quick round of tennis
20 Went astray
24 Andrews or Carvey
28 One of the Ringling brothers
29 "Misery" star
30 Old lab heaters
32 Hear about (with "of")
34 Classic party game
35 Wine holder
36 For grades 1 to 12
38 Cuban article
40 Rag's source of income
43 Fat mouse in "Cinderella"
44 Persian train fares?
45 Kellogg's waffle
46 Kids' rhyme starter
48 Signs off on
49 Boxer's sound

51 More old-fashioned
52 Stock holder
53 Tarzan portrayer's family
56 Robert de ___
57 Trouble constantly
59 Stop
60 Swamp fever symptom
61 Trainee or detainee
62 Impede
64 Birthplace of Penélope Cruz
67 Sister of Terpsichore
69 Watch word
70 Mallorca y Tenerife
72 Blossom support
74 Tar Heel State campus
76 Mamie Eisenhower, ___ Doud
78 "Diff'rent Strokes" actress
79 U.S. tax law book

EXTINCT ANIMALS by Robert A. Doll
The extinct insect at 79-A has been spotted recently in 2007 and 2008.

ACROSS

1 GI garb, for short
5 Blood-typing letters
8 ___ Blue (Danish cheese)
12 Painter Lippo Lippi
15 Oversight
17 2003 Johnny Cash hit
18 "The One I Love" group
19 Extinct cat?
21 Wood sorrel
22 Pigtail, e.g.
23 Pants part
24 Doofus
26 Take a powder
28 Extinct horse?
30 Health
35 Hidden cost, at times
36 Lachrymosity result
37 Length × width = ___
38 Pooh-poohs
40 Divine
41 Crossworder's crutch: Abbr.
42 Not very friendly
43 Princess tormentor
45 Extinct antelope?
51 Paranormal ability
52 Rock of Cashel locale
53 Harvard's Pennypacker Hall, e.g.
55 Mill fodder
59 Dell dude?
61 Creative spark
62 City near Sparks
63 Clean bass
64 Anxiety
66 Extinct fish?
69 Guinness suffix
70 Ravel classic
71 Babe in the woods
74 Minimum
78 "Don't tase me, ___!"
79 Extinct insect?
82 Total jerk
83 Palio course
84 Transfuses
85 "Holy cow!"
86 Artist Magritte
87 Emulate Bode Miller
88 Patty ___

DOWN

1 Search thoroughly
2 From the U.S.
3 Red giant in Cetus
4 Be undecided
5 Go public with
6 "Where the ___ Are" (1960)
7 Grimm beginning
8 Secluded
9 Doggie Daddy's son, familiarly
10 Starbucks option
11 Hoisted, nautically
12 Expressed displeasure
13 Pianist's time to shine
14 Passionate
16 Red Sea republic
20 Stumblebum
25 Former Yugoslav leader
27 Letter abbr.
29 Breathed
30 Roll of bills
31 Mystery writer Ambler
32 Poland's Walesa
33 Ice-cream portion
34 Music genre
39 Less restricted
40 Cumberland ___
44 Come forth
46 Chihuahua checker
47 Part of Einstein's theory
48 For the time being
49 Rich supply
50 Aphrodite's lover
54 Bell and Barker
55 Assortment
56 Moral anguish
57 Nearby
58 Just a little
60 All excited
63 "How Stella Got Her ___ Back" (1998)
65 Speck in the ocean
67 Great passion
68 Dundee denial
72 Cow-headed goddess
73 Depression
75 Au fait
76 Put on eBay
77 Put your big toe in the water
80 One of Alcott's "Little Men"
81 Chi follower

PATCHWORK QUILT   by Brad Wilber
1 Down was first seen as host of the Food Network's "$40 a Day."

ACROSS

1 Hindu avatar
5 Aesop's hare, e.g.
13 They interrupt surfing
16 Impulse transmitter
17 Concha locale
18 Start of three John Wayne movie titles
19 Twinkletoes opposite
20 Come out of hiding
21 Long-jawed fish
22 Paul in "Now, Voyager"
24 "Not ___ million years!"
25 Camp David Accords participant
27 Shoelace tips
28 Unwelcome summer cloud
30 Stick in the fridge
31 Pension law acronym
32 Winless thoroughbred
33 Feudal worker
34 Triangle part
35 African pest caught in cloth traps
37 Some AOL missives
39 Fan sounds
41 Metric wts.
42 West End musical group
47 Bunkers' Queens neighborhood
49 Netherlands queen
50 Noncommittal reply
52 Burlesque prop
53 Russert and Robbins
54 E, on golf leaderboards
55 Come up with
58 Spot fixer?
59 Lebanese designer Elie
62 Duck portrayer in "Peter and the Wolf"
64 Intimate nightclub

66 Karen Carpenter, for one
67 George of "Cheers"
68 Capital of Zimbabwe
69 Pope in 1605
71 As well as
72 Mauritania neighbor
73 Deep Purple frontman Gillan
74 "To Althea, From Prison" poet
77 Yielded
78 White House advisory gp.
79 Not fleshed out
80 Lag b'___ (Jewish holiday)
81 Nice time of year?
82 Certain peerages
83 "I Remember Mama" son

DOWN

1 Dunkin' Donuts pitchwoman
2 Lube from a gun
3 Does double duty, in a way
4 Guitarist Segovia
5 Bullwinkle adversary
6 Had second thoughts about
7 Downed
8 Drew Carey and Mike Myers, e.g.
9 Paintball accessories
10 Make fizzy
11 Scandal sheet
12 Sierra Club logo, essentially
13 Sock pattern

14 It's always relegated to the bottom
15 Noncommittal reply
23 "L'___ c'est moi"
26 Best Supporting Actor of 1982
28 Hoods' pieces
29 Abuse verbally
32 Emmy winner Mullally
36 "Ironweed" setting
38 Kingston Trio hit of 1959
40 Derby of Akron
43 WW2 torpedo vessel
44 "The Weakest Link," for one
45 Marty McFly's specialty
46 Mean Joe Greene, Mel Blount et al.

48 Retrovirus component
51 "Amapola" singer Helen
52 Outdo
56 Rife
57 Israel's first UN delegate
59 Like the Aral Sea
60 Orioles' div.
61 Pronto
63 State animal of 65 Down
65 "Alis volat propriis" state
68 Jimmy Choo trademark
70 Female role in "Spring Awakening"
72 Take for a ride
75 River to the Volga
76 From ___ Z

111 SPLITTING THE . . . by Victor Fleming
We'll let you figure out the rest of the title.

ACROSS

1 Alley denizen
7 Layered haircut
11 Wood that glides in models
16 Creed in "Rocky"
17 Not stay fresh
18 Phillips of "Star Trek: Voyager"
19 Hire, as counsel
20 Designer Gucci
21 Corruption partner
22 Ague, e.g.
24 Water's components, e.g.
25 Fitting worker
26 Caged warbler
27 Kind of guy
31 Spiritual path
32 Rip end
33 Spaced out
36 Short of
37 Ancient Persian poet
41 Key West rental
42 Largest of seven
44 Campfire treat
45 "Got it!"
46 Lack of a key
49 Keydets' sch.
50 Roberto Duran's "I quit!"
52 Drudge of the Web
53 Chinese noodle dish
55 No condensation
56 In need of changing
57 Minoxidil brand name
58 House
60 Spanish sight seer?
62 Tech sch. grad
63 Dress option
66 Bed toppers
69 "___ my case!"
70 Down deep
75 Butler from Charleston
76 Diane Sawyer's birth name
77 Fabled cow owner
78 Vacation rental
79 "Post" page
80 Sartre classic
81 FIVE ARE SPLIT IN THIS PUZZLE

82 Some attendance figs.
83 Minus sign twin

DOWN

1 Maeve Binchy's "___ Road"
2 Vienna-based cartel
3 Caterpillar successor?
4 Potter's supply
5 Elite
6 Tony winner Pinkins
7 Basic food item
8 Big name in hotels
9 Strong devotion
10 Euclidean subj.
11 Cupholder
12 Haphazardly
13 Tibetan capital
14 Less dicey
15 Jittery
23 Slugger Johnny
26 Coquettish
27 1997 Demi Moore title role
28 What a liner may get caught on
29 Japanese floor covering
30 Takes too much of, with "on"
32 Spiced Indian tea
34 Aliases
35 Oxy-5 target
36 Riverbed deposit
38 Occupy
39 Giving guns to
40 "Misery" director
42 Sculpture student's subj.
43 Stood no more
44 Clean Air Act target
47 Broken mirror, say

48 Driver's caution
51 Familiarize
54 Daisy ___ Yokum
56 Retail storefront?
57 Actor's meat
59 Seattle's Best offerings
60 Juice source
61 Internal Islamic battles
63 About
64 Nirvana attainer
65 "___ evil"
66 Unilever brand
67 Butcher shop choice
68 Early Athenian democrat
70 African lily
71 Angry
72 Biological groups
73 ". . . ___ it Memorex?"
74 Jackalope, for one

112 TONSORIAL TUTORIAL by Patrick Jordan
Floyd is the name of the tonsor on 71 Across.

ACROSS

1 Portal uprights
6 Hash browns veggie
10 Word with screen or second
15 Stupid sort
16 Governor's bailiwick
17 Capital in the Andes
18 Mowgli's bear friend
19 Fateful force in Buddhism
20 Drove
21 Opera with a singing barber (with "The")
24 Have the receipt for
25 Puts into the record
26 City near Provo
27 Cause nose-wrinkling
29 Tomato's tinge
30 Agreeably sharp-tasting
32 Bipedal ranch creature
35 Made an effort
37 Dispatches anew
39 Shorthand pro
40 Inventorying aid, briefly
43 Medical suffix
44 Musical with a demonic barber
48 Moslem ruler
51 Tined tools
52 "Frasier" episode, e.g.
56 Some bank collections
58 Vinyl benzene
60 "Mazel ___!"
61 Purposes
63 Pan Am rival, once
64 Appease completely
65 Cutting side
67 Skilled combat pilot
70 Pioneer's house material
71 Sitcom with a folksy barber (with "The")
75 Arledge of "ABC News" fame
76 Certainty
77 Peninsula bordering Israel
79 Near the center
80 Tapped out
81 Shriver's 1978 U.S. Open foe
82 Wind-deposited silt
83 Nolan Ryan's debut team
84 Ralph and Potsie, to the Fonz

DOWN

1 Sloop sail
2 Bruce Wayne portrayer
3 From Italy's second-largest city
4 Insensitive individual
5 Put in a crib, say
6 Brought to Broadway
7 Culinary gadget
8 Highest degree
9 Loath to listen
10 Water pistol discharges
11 Wholesale removal
12 Bone-to-bone connector
13 Road, in old Rome
14 Kerfuffle
16 Did some ice dancing
22 With respect to
23 Precede
24 Metal-bearing minerals
28 Leavenworth locale
31 "I smell ___!"
33 1,501, at the Forum
34 Battleship inits.
36 "That really hurts!"
38 Downy ducks
40 Fingerprinting liquid
41 Wallace in "Cujo"
42 England and Hardin
45 Graphite remover
46 Fluency
47 No longer yielding milk
48 More than capable
49 Day-___ paint
50 Finish (with)
53 Former CBS anchor Harry
54 Contrary to propriety
55 Deprivation
57 Ambushing robbers
58 Bind with a bandage
59 Dash dial
62 "On Language" columnist William
63 Illusionist's repertoire
66 Force units
68 "Otherwise . . ."
69 German industrial hub
71 Seed appendage
72 Preschooler's prohibition
73 SALT concern
74 Place that's buzzing with activity
78 "___ Your Thing": Isley Brothers

113 PRETTY WELL OILED   by Ray Hamel
"Pump Action" was Ray's alternate title.

ACROSS

1 Float easily
5 Give up
13 Bookie alternative
16 First Amendment advocacy grp.
17 Kind of court
18 WWW address
19 Statistical variation
21 Kind of cross
22 Dixie's animated partner
23 French article
24 Use a loom
26 Purplish red
29 Indian River exports
31 Meditation syllables
34 Prefix with state
35 With reluctance
36 Baltic Sea arm
40 Washer's neighbor
41 Prima ballerina
42 Principe, for one
46 Up until today
48 "The View" network
49 Conductor Damrosch
51 Stereotypical gamer
52 Make a gradual transition
55 Birthplace of Gene Autry
56 "Ann Vickers" novelist
58 Jain Temple city
62 Andalusian aunt
63 Jeanne or Bernadette
64 Remember with a poem
65 Bricklayers
68 Watch for
69 Golfer's number
70 Femur spot
74 Dispirited
75 Pasta well-suited for clam sauce?
80 Contact's place
81 One of the Prairie Provinces
82 Bibliography abbr.
83 ID with two hyphens
84 Won over
85 Reagan's Secretary of the Interior

DOWN

1 Mud-daubing insect
2 Curtain opener
3 Linen source
4 Toga alternative
5 Jamaican music
6 "Wag the Dog" ploy
7 Provide
8 William Morris employee
9 Tenuous
10 1967 NHL Rookie of the Year
11 Rock's ___ Fighters
12 Wisconsin's motto
13 Power failure
14 Take a bus
15 Like B.B. King's music
20 "Blade II" director
25 USN rank
27 Dog sound
28 Teeming
29 Track figure
30 Extend a contract
31 Utah city
32 Diving bird
33 More mischievous
35 Singer Keys
37 Chase (off)
38 Source of the Mississippi
39 Big prize in medicine
42 Rival of Jimmy and Bjorn
43 Loads
44 Lawful
45 Wipe away
47 Bruce of "Hill Street Blues"
50 Coca-Cola's home
53 Get a pot going
54 Trivial complaints
56 "I can live with that"
57 Samba city
58 Puts a halt to
59 Without exception
60 Weighted down
61 Modern F/X field
65 Home of the Knights Hospitalers
66 Culet and cuirass
67 Nag
69 Ballet maneuver
71 Crumb
72 Camping nuisance
73 Sword handle
76 Leia's love
77 It may be living or dead
78 Fortas or Burrows
79 Scoundrel

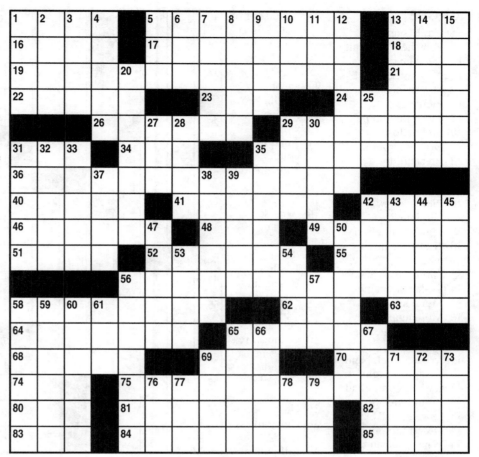

SWELLING RANKS   by Harvey Estes

13 Down can be found in the novel and film "A Clockwork Orange."

ACROSS

1 Circle segments
5 Punishes corporally
11 Get a bead on
16 "___ interesting!"
17 Mysterious
18 Piquancy
19 Eve's first home
20 Mel or Jose
21 Drawing room
22 Be candidly selfless?
25 PIN taker
26 Plenty angry
27 "So long"
28 In more of a hurry
30 "Let's see now, where ___?"
33 Part of a spy name
34 Molecule members
35 Mural site
36 More unusual
37 Eliot protagonist
38 Begin
41 Irritated rock band?
46 Unsightly sights
47 Carbon compound
49 Prom transports
53 "Sister Act" extras
54 Desert bloomers
55 What you can take from me
56 Public relations output
57 Funhouse fixtures
59 Brewer of song
61 Words before camera or rock
62 Pt. of AARP
63 Prize for grouchy kids?
68 Vietnamese capital
69 Not recognized
70 Jump up
72 Eventually become
73 Apartment dweller
74 Very top
75 RBI and ERA
76 Wetland birds
77 Crockpot contents

DOWN

1 Blvd.
2 Republican, by location
3 Vanilla beverage
4 Milli Vanilli's lip action
5 "Thinking of You" singer
6 Like better
7 Very bitter
8 Antidrug agent
9 Patella site
10 Manor worker
11 Analyze for gold
12 Famed Rio beach
13 Korova ___
14 Altar server
15 Kind of reunion
23 Reformer Jacob
24 Baseball card stat
25 Arab of song
29 Fed. agents
30 Combat area
31 Takes in, say
32 Hillside
35 Crumples into a ball
36 USPS beat
38 Crazy like a fox
39 Lilliputian
40 Pkg. purveyor
42 Jennifer Lien's "Voyager" role
43 Goneril's dad
44 Wrong
45 Hunchback's home
48 Mailing to Santa
49 Gate closers
50 Repetitive
51 Daniel Hillard's ex
52 Flare, as nostrils
54 Sticking point
56 Stable staple
57 Fridge stick-on
58 Some computer files
60 Cuts class
61 Rest room sign phrase
64 Holiday period
65 A hundred sawbucks
66 Country in a Beatle song
67 Wistful word
71 Basilica bench

115 JA-PUN-ESE FOOD   by Richard Silvestri
Cry "Yatta!" ("I did it!") after solving this one.

ACROSS

1 String along
7 Surf
12 Bellicose Olympian
16 Walking on air
17 Say "nothin' "
18 Become engaged
19 Gag order at the Japanese restaurant?
21 Sleuthing duo's dog
22 Dedicated lines
23 Crackers or bananas
24 So far
25 "All in the Family" producer
26 Michener epic
29 Place for a dip
31 Pope's emissary
33 Clog
35 Put under
36 Hissy fit at the Japanese restaurant?
40 Use a compass
41 Jersey hangout
42 MPG raters
45 Turku resident
46 Took a load off
49 "Which came first?" thing
51 Political coalition
52 Guitar's little brother
53 Minorca's capital
55 Ear specialist
57 Japanese restaurant song?
62 More clever
65 V-2, for one
66 Battery terminals
67 Someone I remember
68 "Bolero" star
72 Basilica center
73 River of Russia
75 Suffix for self
77 Old greeting
78 Judd's "Taxi" role
79 Spectacle at the Japanese restaurant?
83 Ready to eat
84 Highborn
85 Columbus Day event
86 Ottoman rulers
87 Siouan language
88 Let off the hook

DOWN

1 Stop on a line
2 Slip away from
3 Chicle source
4 Stage actress Hagen
5 Plaines preceder
6 Dutch export
7 Winnow
8 Rumble in the Jungle winner
9 Record material
10 Carmela on "The Sopranos"
11 Colonist
12 Combination
13 Change place cards
14 It's left behind
15 Was generous
20 Key letter
27 Quaker in the woods
28 Phaser setting
30 Milky gem
32 E-mail address ending
34 Scraps for Scrappy-Do
35 Daddy deer
36 Vegan's protein source
37 Composer Satie
38 Hog's word
39 Social-page word
42 "Boola Boola" singers
43 Swanky
44 Broadway opening
47 Child god
48 Greek cross
50 Stare stupidly
51 Savage
54 Gumbo veggie
56 Ready for recycling
57 Quick-reference aids
58 Medieval malediction
59 "Make up your mind!"
60 Name on a slate
61 Internet payment method
62 Dudley Do-Right's home
63 Handy watch?
64 Nine-day devotion
67 Deadly snake
69 Aircraft equipment
70 Get out of
71 In A, e.g.
74 Smart foes
76 Brewery need
80 Taina in "The 39 Steps"
81 Peke's perch
82 Soc. Security supplement

116 MEAN TIME by Patrick Jordan
"The First Lady of the Theater" can be found at 19 Across.

ACROSS

1 Donkeys' ancestors
6 Corp. chiefs
10 Parts of putters
16 Far from firm
17 "Six" prefix
18 Thick stew
19 **Speaker of quip**
21 Execute excessively
22 Chum
23 Sovereign's topper
25 Mary in "The Maltese Falcon"
26 "How sweet ___!"
28 Word with canal or candy
29 Fess (up)
31 Choleric emotion
32 **Quip: Part 1**
37 In ___ (at heart)
38 Mythical bowman
39 Some hooded snakes
42 Brown-coated ermine
45 Prepare French toast
46 Denver's elevation, famously
47 Sphere at a coronation
48 **Quip: Part 2**
52 Apply blades to blades?
53 "Crossroads of the South Pacific"
55 Verbal fanfares
56 Certain sport shirts
58 Tomahawks and such
59 One who watches
60 Calcutta cover-up
62 **Quip: Part 3**
68 AOL exchanges
70 Innermost pt.
71 Sampan propeller
72 Rosalind of "M*A*S*H"
73 Heart
75 Small herding dog
79 Superlative syllable
80 Graduated
82 **Quip: Part 4**
84 Make the scene
85 Tofu source
86 "Three Tall Women" playwright
87 Kind of line to sign
88 Zoning director's map
89 Elegantly attired

DOWN

1 Barbecue receptacle
2 Close-fitting dress
3 ___ Mae (student loan agency)
4 Make last (with "out")
5 Coordinate, colloquially
6 Pretense
7 Pooh's gloomy chum
8 Yoked team
9 Freelancer's encl.
10 Initials that delight angels
11 Castro's capital
12 Grows gray-haired
13 Loudly, to Liszt
14 Elizabeth I's dynasty
15 Keep in a crib, say
20 Gardeners, on occasion
24 Camry company
27 Where Namath played
30 Bremen's river
33 ___ spumante
34 Shore dinner, e.g.
35 Squares up
36 Edward Jones Dome athlete
40 Trudge
41 Plies a needle
42 Davenport or settee
43 Fruity Pebbles rival
44 Decorative collectibles
45 Audiocassette marking
49 1945 Alamogordo event, briefly
50 Parfait features
51 Gaelic speaker's homeland
54 Suffix for shrew
57 Multivitamin metal
60 Tries to smack
61 Condor's quarters
63 Eight-note interval
64 "See? I wasn't lyin'!"
65 "Inside ___" (TNT postgame show)
66 Holy Saturday follower
67 "Wait a bit longer"
68 Blue line
69 Brewery or biology prefix
74 Buttonhole, for one
76 Fastening gadget
77 Organic compound
78 Perón and Marie Saint
81 Mars's hue
83 Stately shader

117 ON THE TABLE   by Arlan and Linda Bushman
60 Across are the sources of many bumper snickers.

ACROSS

1 Impassive
7 Flinch
10 Small firecrackers
16 IVP dye
17 Cobbler
18 Overseas travel option
19 North Dakota's "Sunflake City"
21 Comb obstruction
22 "Yo!"
23 Chilling
24 Off-road ride, for short
25 Antediluvian
26 On the nose
27 1943 penny material
29 EPA concern
32 Giant upset of 2008
37 Serbian President Tadic
39 Uniform
40 Cookie fresh-baked in 1912
41 Tabletop griller
44 Kind of shark
47 Aussie swimmer Thorpe
48 Ace of clubs
51 Weeks per annum
52 Flavor
53 Taciturn
55 Religious image
57 Eastern ties
59 Set down
60 Conceits of car owners
65 ___ buco
66 "American Pie" locale
67 Rite site
69 Spree
72 Game pieces
73 Sound of displeasure
74 Char's tote
77 Brusque
79 Wimbledon trophies
81 Krypton, for one
82 Word of support
83 Official count
84 Milne moper
85 Tread softly
86 Frank's comic-strip pal

DOWN

1 Exhale audibly
2 Sped
3 Jazz singer Anita
4 Memorial designer Maya
5 Book section
6 Checkmate
7 Brownies
8 Boost
9 Thumbs-up
10 Parlor piece
11 Tremble
12 Pedestal topper
13 Emilia's treacherous mate
14 Visor
15 Husky haul
20 Its players know the score: Abbr.
24 In danger
26 To her, some things are "loverly"
27 Describe concisely
28 Wall St. deal
29 Decline
30 Napoleon's birthplace
31 Address
33 Wine concoction
34 Lines up
35 Fatigues
36 First name in horror films
38 Salutation word
42 Greek vowel
43 Unwrap hurriedly
45 Waiting rm. locale
46 Behold, to Livy
49 Chivalrous
50 Deck with laurels
51 Tyler in "Lord of the Rings"
54 ___-Magnon
56 Goose egg
58 Ravenous
61 Strengthen metal
62 Mimieux of movies
63 62 Down's "Time Machine" role
64 Posture
68 Incense
69 Wisecrack
70 Competent
71 Overcast
73 Featured Prado artist
74 Dwell on
75 Comics penguin
76 Attention getter
78 Kids' card game
79 Once around
80 TV info source

118 "GIVE ME SOME 79 DOWN!" by Victor Fleming
A breathtaking experience!

ACROSS

1 Hitter of 61 in '61
6 Influences
11 One who shoots hoops
16 Former Italian queen
17 Golfer Baddeley
18 Half a '60s dance
19 Numeric leader?
20 Seat of Siskiyou County, California
21 Battery part
22 Where to find tom yum
25 "A vote for ___ a vote for . . ."
26 Slangy refusal
27 Ford make, for short
28 Polite title
31 Part of ETA
32 Literally, "for this"
34 Ricardo, to Mertz
36 Robins' homes
38 Delight
41 Cleo of jazz
42 Brinker in books
45 Folk forename
47 Makes angry
48 "Barney's Version" author
52 Gander or bull
53 ___ City, Baghdad
54 End of a fitting phrase
55 "Fleas" poet Nash
57 Garage item
59 Words of clarification
63 Brandy Norwood role
65 Cutting light
68 Inflation meas.
69 Spanish guitarist (1778–1839)
70 Composition of some beds
73 Spring resort
74 "I cannot tell ___"
75 NOW president (1991–2001)
79 Briskly
81 Words after get or grab
82 Charley Weaver's hometown
83 Figure skater Slutskaya
84 De Gaulle's birthplace
85 "Okie From Muskogee" singer Haggard
86 "Bertha" composer Ned
87 Nuremberg defendant
88 Musical upbeats

DOWN

1 Butcher
2 Roll call report, perhaps
3 Fixings
4 "It's ___ Kiss": Cher
5 Coal-rich German region
6 Follows the doctor's order
7 Pumbaa in "The Lion King"
8 Field
9 Pansy of Dogpatch
10 Deadfall
11 Pulpit's locale
12 Uncle's partner
13 French word list
14 Days of yore
15 Ham holder
23 Quash
24 Former "Jeopardy" host Fleming
29 Central
30 I-40 and I-30
32 "It's ___ state of affairs!"
33 Kaleidocolors maker
35 Executed perfectly
37 Triplets
39 Do something human
40 Chicago Cubs manager (1982–83)
43 Big inits. in video games
44 Improvise vocally
46 World Series mo.
48 Cartoon "Mr."
49 First glasses, e.g., comparatively
50 Busyness
51 Will beneficiary
52 May day honorees
56 Blue Jackets, e.g.
58 Louisiana namer
60 Filled pastries
61 Turning point
62 Tinted tees
64 Alpine river
66 "Eek!" producer
67 Wax producer
71 Perfume bottles
72 ___ off the old block
74 Russian republic
76 Teen concern
77 One loved by Hercules
78 Spice Girls member
79 WORD FOUND IN 8 ANSWERS
80 In favor of

119 WORD SALAD   by Doug Peterson
3 Down was the second American to fly in space.

ACROSS

1 Convertible, colloquially
7 Mount in Exodus
12 Qualified
16 Moon of Jupiter
17 Stiff jacket feature
19 Body-shop application
20 Unbelievable
21 ___Tafari
22 Lincoln, in a Whitman poem
24 Drops in a mailbox
25 Otherwise
27 Ivy League member
28 Gnu group
29 Disheveled one
30 Wine lover's prefix
31 1945 conference site
34 Stock-ticker sights
36 Natasha's negative
38 Grp. with a noted journal
39 Divided into installments
41 "See ya!"
43 Where Reno was once located
47 Developed
48 Court, in a way
49 Pops
50 Bakery purchase
51 "SNL" alum Joe
55 Jubilance
58 ___ arms (outraged)
60 One of Donald's nephews
61 Saturates
62 Howlin' Wolf's music
63 LAX listings
64 Bradley and Epps
66 Beckons
68 Merlot holder
69 Superman's home
71 Camden Yards player
73 Place-setting piece
74 Hammock user
75 "Ol' Man River" composer
76 They may be spliced
77 Urban two-wheelers

DOWN

1 Quash
2 How music is sensed
3 Project Mercury astronaut
4 Alley prowler
5 Crude acronym?
6 Like some mirrors
7 "Miracle on 34th Street" director George
8 Capra classic set in Bedford Falls, NY
9 Away from home
10 Before too long
11 Post-op stop
12 Thicket trees
13 Risky social arrangement
14 Finish a flight
15 Work units
18 First signs
23 Keeps trying
26 Walt Alston's 1955 home
28 On a roll
31 Dixie desserts
32 "You said it!"
33 Trade center
35 Taylor tyke of reruns
37 Pained cry
40 Halls of music
41 Old Ford models
42 Oscar winner in "Cocoon"
43 Shade of green
44 Orenburg's river
45 Seltzer-bottle liquid
46 Gullywasher
50 ___ Gatos, CA
52 Defeat at the polls
53 Propelled a Schwinn
54 Pearl harborers
56 Earthling, in sci-fi novels
57 "There, there"
59 Signs of life
62 Ina in films
64 Siberian metropolis
65 Apportion
66 Volcano top
67 Milkshake flavor
70 USPS parcel
72 DSL co.

COAUTHOR   by Buddy Richard
Joseph Conrad's "Heart of Darkness" was the basis for "Apocalypse Now."

ACROSS
1 Now companion
5 "Immediately!"
9 They're obvious
16 "Houston, ___ got a problem!"
17 "The Night They Invented Champagne" musical
18 "You are ___, sir" (McMahon line)
19 **Joseph Conrad quotation: Part I**
21 Further from rational
22 Caravel of Columbus
23 ___'acte
25 Laughable
26 "Angela's Ashes," e.g.
28 Spenserian verb
31 La-la intro
32 **Quotation: Part II**
36 "Favorite" relation
38 Bishop's bailiwick
39 Ugly sights
40 Relative of a Salchow
42 Seattle's Best brew
45 Birthplace of Saint Ignatius
48 **Quotation: Part III**
49 Rumor unit, perhaps
53 Ranked a tourney differently
56 Convenience for an ed.
57 Illustrative story
60 ER figures
63 "Care for a spot of ___?"
64 **Quotation: Part IV**
68 USN petty officer
69 "Cats" poet
70 Try again
73 Torch's work
76 Long ago, long ago
78 Give to
79 1997 Hawke movie
82 **Quotation: Part V**
84 Rome description
85 Choice
86 Zaire's Mobutu ___ Seko

87 Have an effect
88 FCC concerns
89 System that can improve your image?

DOWN
1 Afternoon hr.
2 Figure skater known as "The Golden Girl"
3 Betting phrase
4 Calculus inventor
5 Amt. on a 1040
6 Web locale
7 Conference need
8 Browning product
9 It merged with AT&T in 1999
10 Howard or Turcotte
11 Bearish start
12 Where rials are spent
13 Dole or Pryor
14 Three-time Wimbledon champ
15 They may be winning or losing
20 Train company stocks
24 Ring leader?
27 Bar choice
29 Lid annoyance
30 "If ___ walls could talk . . ."
33 Start of a laugh
34 She, in Salerno
35 Embarrassing guests
36 "Old pal" of song
37 Kitchen utensils maker
41 TV producer Michaels
43 Metallic marble
44 Third degree?
46 Groucho's grimace

47 TV's "___ World Turns"
50 Chumpish
51 Apply
52 Pastureland
54 Series ender
55 Orthodontist's deg.
57 Neptune's photographer
58 Repeat
59 Wrote for another
61 JEC successor
62 Warfare tactic
65 Former justice Abe
66 Sweater's remark
67 Beat
71 "For every Bird ___": Dickinson
72 Episc. title
74 Other, to Ochoa
75 Half of Mork's greeting
77 Ride herd on
80 Curbside container
81 City council rep.
83 ___ publica

"DON'T ASK ME Y" by Billie Truitt
59 Across is the subject of many New Year's resolutions!

ACROSS

1 Post-injury program
6 Lover of Daphnis
11 British sitcom, for short
16 Cookbook author Prudhomme
17 Common letter sign-off
18 Worth
19 Where a browbeater goes shopping?
21 More than annoyed
22 Palindromic "before"
23 Gingerbread house nibbler
24 Trust
25 Helen of Troy's mother
27 Even score
28 Pretentious
29 Prepare a treatise on a card game?
33 Copier problem
36 Make certain
38 "Lord, ___?": Matt. 26:22
39 Exist as a group
40 Tampa neighbor, briefly
41 Piece of land
42 Hobbyist's knife brand
44 Have ___ with (know somebody)
45 Beat decisively
48 Distort
49 "The Count of ___ Cristo"
51 Plains native
52 Edmondton team
54 Man of the future
55 Shiny balloon material
57 Kind of bond
58 Moreover
59 Part of a rotund silhouette?
61 "No restrictions ___ kind!"
63 Geisha's sash
64 Go by
68 Sporty scarves
70 Dutch beer brand
73 Whirlpool tub
74 Occupy, as a table
75 Very dirty field hand?
77 Bikini, notably
78 "The Tortoise and the Hare" author
79 Make better
80 Prize money
81 So last year
82 Movie producer Carlo

DOWN

1 Revolting one?
2 Toughen
3 Sank, as a putt
4 The whole enchilada
5 Birch or Evan of Indiana
6 Popular poison in whodunnits
7 Rocking toy, to a tot
8 Gospel writer
9 Hurler Hershiser
10 Ballpark fig.
11 Amelia Earhart, for one
12 Old dance sites
13 Parka worn by a dandruff sufferer?
14 Mobile beginning
15 "___ there, done that!"
20 Ripens
24 Cherokee Sal's creator Harte
26 Go-ahead
28 Japanese watchdog
30 Boy king of ancient Egypt
31 Expose to public scorn
32 "___ Mio"
34 Main line
35 Cat chorus
36 When two hands meet
37 Porcupine with a medical degree?
40 Brazilian dance
41 Bit of potpourri
43 Out
46 Yuletide greenery
47 Messenger
50 Prepare for war
53 Robbins of Baskin-Robbins
56 Longings
57 Group within a group
60 The whole enchilada
62 Stable infants
65 Skier's vacation spot
66 Used up
67 Famed New York restaurateur
68 On the double
69 Part of LASIK
70 Bailiwick
71 America or Manners
72 Type of year
75 Mountain pass
76 Latin lover's verb

122

ACROSS

1 Hands-on noshes
6 Blockbuster
11 Arugula dish
16 Stand by
17 Frayed
18 Hirsch of "Into the Wild"
19 Sinbad, for one?
22 Monk title
23 Inexperienced one
24 Pastry concoction
25 ASCAP rival
26 Give a cheer
28 Ditto
30 Sorting station
33 Crafty
36 Deck number
37 What Boris Karlof made?
45 Deceive
46 Zest source
47 Berberian of opera
48 Symphony member
49 Noted translation software
52 Surveyor's map
53 Key preposition
54 Increase
55 Sicily neighbor
56 Getting bonked on the head by an apple?
61 Galoot
62 Cabinet find
63 Food on sticks
68 NFLer Manning
69 Olden days
73 Words of praise
74 City on the Oka
76 DDE's opponent
78 Caesar of comedy
79 Sheep and geese mixed together?
84 Betelgeuse home
85 Place
86 Rouse
87 ___ Martin Lagonda Ltd.
88 Bar serving amounts
89 Gathering storm

DOWN

1 Boardwalk treat
2 Mindful
3 Ring of plotters
4 Flax derivative
5 Rung
6 Visit briefly
7 "Spy vs. Spy" magazine
8 Working hard
9 Vapor
10 Many-headed monster
11 Bishop's domain
12 Doc bloc
13 Pole dance
14 Historic mission
15 Coarse cloth
20 Flat-topped hill
21 English blue cheese
27 Cafe order
29 Couple's possessive
31 Describe in detail
32 Sugarloaf setting
34 Pi follower
35 Frog hangout
37 Emotionally reserved
38 Journalist's worry
39 Arrowsmith's wife
40 Firm up
41 Ins. option
42 "My Eyes Adored You" singer
43 Versifier's muse
44 "Paradise Lost" figure
49 Jester
50 Director Lee
51 Prickly husk
52 Easy mark
54 Course

55 Astronaut Jemison
57 Prevailed
58 Compete
59 Keys
60 Fence's supplier
63 Warming quaff
64 Spray target
65 Send payment
66 Mastery
67 Donnybrook
70 Levant of levity
71 ___-Tikki-Tavi
72 Car with a "horsecollar" grille
75 Stead
77 Sharp rebuke
80 Casper's comment
81 Wayfarer's spot
82 Galley need
83 In arrears

123 MONOGRAM MEMBERS by John Underwood
. . . and all these monograms have two things in common.

ACROSS

1 HCH member
6 JEC member
10 JQA member
16 Lash of old westerns
17 Allies' adversary
18 Sci-fi author Le Guin
19 Man from Muscat
20 Satirized (with "up")
21 Bread maker?
22 WGH member
24 FDR member
25 Degrees for attys.
26 Perfume the air
27 Fishy bunch
31 Gov. Landon et al
32 Polygraph flunker
36 "___ a Symphony": Supremes
37 Road on a Beatles album
39 Objets d'art
40 "Beetle Bailey" creator Walker
41 Verdi's "___ Miller"
42 Like the Riddler
43 Vet
44 WJC member
46 Saint in Brazil
47 Left port
49 1300 hours
50 Sampling of opinions
51 Jimmy of the "Daily Planet"
52 Capital of Ghana
53 Swab the deck again
54 "Little" kid of comics
55 Wings
56 Nephew of King Arthur
57 Sherpa's home
59 The sun as deity
61 LBJ member
63 RBH member
68 Two-person bike
69 Neutron's locale
71 Frat pledge persecutor
72 "Truth ___?" (party game)

73 Storm
74 Lose ground
75 RWR member
76 JKP member
77 DDE member

DOWN

1 Wooden shoe
2 One-L priest
3 Composer Khachaturian
4 ___ fever
5 Lake Wobegon creator
6 Gently maneuvered (into)
7 Jumps for Mao Asada
8 ___ Tin Tin
9 D-day amphibian
10 Shea Stadium locale
11 Russian range
12 El Al passengers
13 Former Georgia senator
14 Advertising award
15 "Babi ___": Yevtushenko
23 Indisposed
24 Hang tough
26 More sharply defined
27 USG member
28 Bach work
29 Act of derring-do
30 Granola bar bit
31 Truancy
33 Exasperating
34 Pigged out
35 GRF member
37 "___ Wiedersehen!"
38 Like some glasses
39 Horse transport
41 Called the shots
42 Tattoo honoree
44 Aniston, familiarly

45 Watering place
48 Spartan king killed at Thermopylae
50 By means of
52 "'Tis a pity!"
53 Worked on the Southfork
55 Prehistoric primates
56 "Blimey!"
58 Calendario leaf
59 From the beginning
60 American watch company
61 Italian Adriatic port
62 S ___ (thrift)
64 ___-kiri
65 World's shallowest sea
66 ___-Mix Concrete
67 Harriet Beecher Stowe book
68 Sugarbush lift
69 Ham's refuge
70 "The Bonesetter's Daughter" author

QUESTIONABLE CLUES by Bonnie L. Gentry
Clues with question marks signify puns . . . as you'll soon discover.

ACROSS

1 Addition sign?
6 Acid head?
11 Horsepower source?
15 Iron product?
17 Separatist?
18 Ltr. of approval?
19 Fixed one's eyes?
20 John Hancock site?
22 Part of a return address?
23 Castle with a lot of steps?
25 Spade for digging up dirt?
26 Sweet ending?
27 Those who shouldn't live in glass houses?
29 Do a hair-raising job?
33 Steps along the Seine?
35 India Inc.?
36 Digital window?
38 Check mate?
40 Movie trailer?
41 Quick draw?
42 Took the cake?
43 Taken in by a doctor?
44 Is on the bottom?
45 Red plot?
50 Match ends?
51 Middle sax?
52 Is for two people?
53 The dark side?
54 Gets better?
55 The high cost of leaving?
60 One who's always off?
62 Non-ewe?
63 Make-up name?
64 Dig deeply?
65 Meter maid?
68 Self starter?
69 The same partner?
71 Eau de Cologne?
72 Better this than dead?
73 High jink?
77 Key rings?
80 Knight time?
81 Supreme leader?
82 Bus stations?
83 Welfare state?
84 Passes notes?
85 All-night bar?

DOWN

1 Emergency measures?
2 Exhibi-tionist?
3 Go bumper to bumper with?
4 Canal zones?
5 Follower of Mao?
6 Like some firm elbows?
7 Brought up the rear?
8 Lay low?
9 Mariners' catcher?
10 Lucky strikes?
11 Well-invested group?
12 The start of it all?
13 Soldier material?
14 Church lady?: Abbr.
16 Text massage?
21 Social activist?
24 Part of a stage?
26 Poetic ego-booster?
27 Mattress handle?
28 Cry before dinner?
30 Tall story?
31 Deep place?
32 Thought patterns?
34 Acts hawkish?
37 Foreign correspondent?
39 Bad-smelling flower?
40 A Bonn vivant?: Abbr.
43 Smash letters?
44 Flower holders?
45 Had a peak experience?
46 Scout master?
47 Remove the dirt from?

48 They're out of this world?
49 Butter up?
50 Banks with style?
54 Magic place?
55 Old green coats?
56 Closing on Sunday?
57 Moor jealous?
58 Shot putters?
59 Law closing?
61 Attended to pressing needs?
62 Work on moving pictures?
66 Church keys?
67 Parking place?
70 Tight positions?
72 Mechanical starter?
73 Thesis intro?
74 Do ground work?
75 Shortly before?
76 Crowd in old Rome?
78 Main man?
79 Flightless bird?

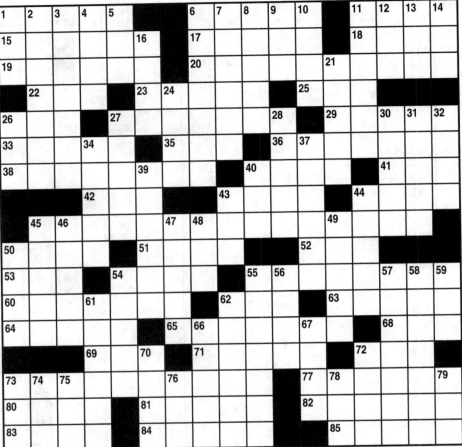

125 THE GOOD, THE BAD, AND THE UGLY   by Martha C. Patty
21 Down wasn't that bad. It climbed to #1 in the UK charts in 1963.

ACROSS

1 Ishmael's father
8 "No ___"
12 Moses in a 1971 Jerry Reed song
16 "Il Trovatore" heroine
17 Mythical Hun king
18 Shetland's tail?
19 Amazing
20 Told lies about
22 Bivouac item
23 Tribunal of old Israel
24 December 31
26 Sheer fabric
27 Go ___ for
31 Toe woe
32 Before deadline
33 1950 Isaac Asimov work
35 Kind of council
37 Sensation of mistrust
39 Drool
44 Start of a backwoods opinion
45 Like many classical aphorisms
46 One after another
48 UGLY feud
49 Zero
51 Popular mint
52 Like some traffic
56 Threat extremes?
58 Hybrid garment
59 Reduce to a pulp
60 Like a hungry lion
62 Singer Humperdinck
64 Mrs. John Quincy Adams et al.
69 Determined to have
70 Ape
71 Reader of crosswords?
72 "___ Marlene" (1944 song)
73 Places where hits are taken
74 Model
75 Acid-resistant wood
76 DNA component

DOWN

1 College grad
2 Nota ___
3 Phoenix kin
4 Anthologies
5 GOOD 1993 Parton/Lynn/Wynette album
6 Golfer Palmer, informally
7 Rival acquired by Whirlpool
8 Rubber
9 Stephen King's "Hearts in ___"
10 "... ___ flowing with milk and honey": Ex. 3:8
11 Ho Chi ___
12 Tarzan's realm
13 "Tuesdays With ___": Albom
14 "Strange Interlude" playwright
15 Gateway to Australia
21 BAD Elvis Presley song
25 "The Godfather" composer
27 Conical homes
28 "___ Ben Jonson!": Young
29 Termite, say
30 Old adders
32 Skill
34 Tastelessly affected
36 Kind of coat
38 Monogram ltr.
40 Former White Sox owner Bill
41 A hard ___ follow
42 13th-century invader
43 Opposite of kill
47 RAZR company
48 Angle
50 Slob's opposite
52 Accelerated
53 Locate on the dial
54 They may be vital
55 South Carolina river
57 Flint is a form of it
60 Even the score again
61 One for whom all roads lead to roam
63 It goes to waist
65 "Put ___ writing!"
66 ___-Flush
67 Heaps
68 Zaire's Mobutu ___ Seko

ACROSS

1 Interior
6 Increases the kitty
13 Least bit
16 Like a loud crowd
17 Do voice-over work
18 Luau instrument, briefly
19 Barrel maker in an Alberta city?
21 Discovery docked with it in 1997
22 Intertwine
23 Trunk topper
24 Dark brown hue
26 Branco or Bravo preceder
27 Called one's own
29 Web surfer's stop
32 Further
33 Gave a pitch
36 Bearing protuberances
38 Empire with a sedative effect?
42 Entr'___
45 Servitude symbol
46 "Spring forward" abbr.
47 "It just came to me!"
48 Caroler's leapers
50 Make a miscue
52 Exxon ship
54 Priest in I Samuel
55 Superman's nemesis Luthor
58 Passport verification
61 E-mail command
62 Fortress built from Italian turnovers?
66 Mexican-American man
67 Stupid sort
70 Ear cleaner brand
72 Apply crudely
74 ___ Na Na (Woodstock group)
75 Daily grind
77 Acknowledged the bride's entrance
79 Breathtaking serpent?
81 Graphite eradicator
83 "Glass Bell" novelist Anaïs
84 Amateur criminal's mug shot?
88 Pixel
89 Removed by plucking
90 Dressed to the ___
91 Baseball bat wood
92 Unity
93 Antiquing chemicals

DOWN

1 Mugger repeller, perhaps
2 Shah's subjects, once
3 Sour cream serving
4 Icelandic epic
5 Windpipe
6 "___ way you slice it"
7 Table salt, chemically
8 Three, in Toulouse
9 Crumbling away
10 Tree tapper's collection
11 Salt Lake City athlete
12 Cuzco's country
13 Fund-raising event
14 Steinbeck's Joad family, e.g.
15 ___ Haute, Indiana
20 "Cross my heart!"
25 Butte's larger kin
28 Garage band's sample
30 Barbarous barber Sweeney
31 Haagen Dazs rival
34 Cooled with cubes
35 Irrigation barrier
37 Aware of
39 Moxie
40 At that point
41 Gridiron division
42 1964 Tony winner Guinness
43 Pop machine option
44 Infinitesimal fraction
49 Parking meter feature
51 Witty comment
53 Realization remark
56 Town on the Chisholm Trail
57 Lucy Lawless role
59 Briny bodies
60 Pollen producer
63 Microwaves
64 Tunnel center?
65 "My ___" (1979 hit for The Knack)
68 Garlicky poison gas
69 Swordsman with a second
70 Press conf. segment
71 The Supremes et al.
73 "Hooch"
76 Lengthy lock
78 Morph or plasm prefix
80 Inspires wonder
82 "I don't give ___!" ("Who cares?")
85 Oat bristle
86 "School Daze" director Spike
87 HQs for some sgts.

127 "I'M IN!" by Richard Silvestri
This is one title to take literally.

ACROSS

1 Explorer, for one
4 "The ___ Girls" (2001 Sorvino film)
9 Disharmony
15 Sixteen-wheeler
16 Beat, in a way
17 String along
18 Minuet movement
19 First name in makeup
20 Shake down
21 Actual approximation?
24 City on the Humboldt
25 Print-shop worker
26 At an angle
28 Rustic
32 Daniel Boone's brother
33 Grounded flyer
36 Bank depositor's facial expression?
40 Part of a foot
44 Lehigh and Lafayette, e.g.
45 Wouk work
46 Biblical dancer
48 Anticipatory time
49 ___ too many (gets drunk)
50 Spud spot
51 Brace
53 "Jurassic Park" beast
54 Question asked of a charades player?
57 Annapolis grad.
58 Part of R&R
59 "Damn Yankees" team
64 Undivided
67 Crow home
68 Pamplona runner
71 Dentistry as a hobby?
75 Military command
77 Shout from the stands
78 Takeover action
79 Guru
80 Gold standard
81 Mem. of the bar
82 Size up
83 Twisting
84 ___ Moines

DOWN

1 Sister of Venus
2 Kayak cousins
3 End of the rainbow?
4 Top four
5 Rigging attachment
6 Hostile to
7 Abounds
8 Noted toy company
9 Woody Allen film
10 Animator Avery
11 Put on a scale?
12 Cult figure
13 Bifurcate
14 Opposite of ecto-
15 Bacon bit
22 Little lust boy?
23 Iceman's aid
27 Minneapolis suburb
29 Pink in the middle
30 Bird, in combinations
31 As-it's-happening broadcast
33 Delight in
34 It's part of the act
35 Fax forerunner
37 ". . . ruler of the Queen's ___" G&S
38 Flashes of light
39 75%, perhaps
40 Private lines
41 Troublesome gas
42 Argil and kaolin
43 Sounds of merriment
47 Beat one's breast
49 Song of praise
51 Path starter
52 Cast object
55 Athletic awards
56 Grub
60 Foursome
61 Narcotic sedative
62 Slackens
63 Like a dive
64 Fill with joy
65 Part of a drink order
66 One of the Allens
68 The Crimson Tide
69 Western tribe
70 Glasses glass
72 Consort of Zeus
73 It's all downhill from here
74 Affectedly aesthetic
76 Lusitania's call

GROUCHO THE CRITIC   by Ed Early
14-D will always be remembered for the catch he made in the 1954 World Series.

ACROSS

1 Salutary clubs
5 Car sticker stat
8 DDE
11 High-end cheese
15 "Felicity" star Russell
16 Ends up in a padded cell
18 Home of Wyeth's "Christina's World"
19 **Start of a Groucho review**
22 Free-for-all
23 Piston great Thomas
24 Electrical units
25 **Part 2 of review**
28 Sedative
31 Jeremy's "Entourage" role
32 1975 Isabelle Adjani title role
36 Stove burner?
37 Heathrow arrival of yore
38 Wright in "The Steel Trap"
39 ___ in Charles
40 Four Monopoly sqs.
42 Dancer Lili Saint-___
43 Hydroplane support
44 Miss Brockovich
46 **Part 3 of review**
50 Strong ___ ox
51 Edward James in "Stand and Deliver"
53 "Let me repeat . . ."
54 "Palookaville" actor Adam
55 Western director Sergio
56 "Long time ___"
57 Klemperer and Preminger
58 **Part 4 of review**
61 Waxman in "Hollywood Ending"
62 Observe
63 **End of review**
72 Charlie of early whodunits
73 Desperate
74 Green cup
76 Injured
77 Monkey's uncle?
78 ___ lot (very little)
79 March time
80 Trying one?
81 Telephone service

DOWN

1 No-fat milk
2 Ending for milli-
3 Nutmeg skin
4 Court huddle
5 Exec. level
6 Kind of sci.
7 Japanese entertainers
8 "This is no joke!"
9 Blues singer McDonald
10 Icelandic letter
11 Authorize
12 Barbie or Ken
13 Amo, amas, ___
14 "Say Hey Kid" of baseball
17 They enjoy the slope
20 Spay
21 Tax scofflaw
26 "Three's Company" nurse
27 Part man, part goat
28 Seminole chief
29 Dove for gems
30 "I, Robot" author's memoir
33 Rent
34 Boomer of football
35 Kind of raceway
41 "Goosebumps" author
42 Relinquished
45 Much ado about nothing
47 Lake Placid org.
48 Part of Ovid's name
49 ___ Bien Phu, Vietnam
50 "Begin the Beguine" clarinetist
52 Glacial pinnacle
54 "When I take my Sugar ___"
59 Mire
60 "As God is my judge!"
63 It's usually dull
64 Hounds' prey
65 Aussie animals
66 Ivan who produced "Gog"
67 Sutherland solo
68 Without purpose
69 Khartoum river
70 Tucson college, briefly
71 Developer's layout
72 Sorority letter
75 UFO passengers

ACROSS

1 Gathering of politicians, informally
11 Printing goof
17 Comment on a tedious trip
18 Dugout items
19 Some models
20 Ring source
21 Pt. of AARP
22 "Ah me!"
23 Asmara's land
24 June portrayer
26 Elev.
27 Indian export
28 Give it a go
29 Next to bat
31 Items sent to record companies
33 Checked item
34 Plug away
36 McKellen in "The Da Vinci Code"
37 It's in the soup but hard to chew
38 Light wood
41 Vieira's show
43 Seasonal numbers
44 Classic children's song
47 Tired writer?
49 Just
50 Tart
52 Object in a courtroom
53 Best example
54 Cold response
55 West Wing worker
58 Straight up
59 Was lost in thought
61 "Pretty nice!"
65 Gallery objects
66 Syr. and Eg., once
67 Sharer's word
69 One of the Marxes
70 Earns
72 Small detail?
74 Where to spend a kip
75 Sorrowful cry
76 Pig out, e.g.
78 Rent collector
79 Eclectic magazine
80 Will's subject
81 Private talks

DOWN

1 Sporty Chevy
2 Up
3 Prepared for a blow
4 Matching pair
5 Lush locale
6 Place of fiction
7 Longtime Dolphins coach
8 Official messenger
9 Aeschylus trilogy
10 Horror director Craven
11 Cuts ridges into
12 Craze
13 Body of soldiers
14 One way to sell
15 Winner at Bull Run
16 Examination prose
23 College on the Thames
25 "The Name of the Rose" writer
30 Pool
32 Waffler's answer
33 Complain constantly
35 Fortune
37 Back muscle
38 Letter clarification
39 Old calculators
40 Weary traveler's cry
42 Sweetie pies
43 Room on board
45 Words before arms
46 Conduit bend
48 Cooperstown stat
51 Chimney deposit
54 Make, as CDs
56 "How dumb of me!"
57 Latin list shortener
59 D preceder
60 Circle in Washington
62 Former German chancellor Willy
63 High point
64 Medicine givers
66 ". . . lead ___ into temptation . . ."
68 Big name in "Chicago"
71 Bart Simpson sister
73 Fame's Irene
76 Kind of instinct
77 Rouge or noir

130 A SHORT WEEK   by Edgar Fontaine
A clever challenger from this native New Englander.

ACROSS

1 Post sans postage
6 Actress Freeman
10 Volcanic rock
16 Bicyclist Armstrong
17 Leave out
18 Muse of astronomy
19 Interminable on d 6?
21 Rag
22 Most stick-in-the-mud
24 Strain
25 Pawn
28 Genteel affair
29 For each one
31 Glutton on d 5?
33 Overlooked
36 Cultivated land
37 Blaspheme
41 Hang in loose folds
42 Moonshine's Irish kin
44 Ration
46 "Irish" Meusel of baseball
47 Milano Mr. on d 2?
50 Pain in the neck
54 "___ Davis Eyes"
55 Pulpits
60 Misbehave
62 Advisers of old
64 Invisible emanations
65 Make right
67 Secure on d 4?
69 Luanda's land
71 Part of USSR
72 Caustic substances
73 Negligible amount
75 Bones of the spinal column
78 Attach anew
80 Hot on d 1?
84 Safe and sound
85 Clarinet's cousin
86 Noted Barton
87 Ramada chain, e.g.
88 School misfit
89 Matches, as tracks

DOWN

1 Ernie Keebler, e.g.
2 Spoil the finish
3 "Wheel of Fortune" buy
4 Move like Midori
5 Period after Mardi Gras
6 Shapers
7 Longines rival
8 Not absolute
9 Perplexed
10 Meddle
11 Notre Dame first name
12 Make out on d 7?
13 Civil War battle site
14 Norseman Ericsson
15 Not at all sweet
20 Overdo the TLC
23 Goad
25 Web address start
26 Miami or Lima location
27 Beantown center?
30 Hail Mary target
32 Those people
34 Starting center?
35 Second smallest st.
38 Pine away
39 Type type
40 Notorious Hiss
43 Head, slangily
45 Rocky crag
48 Cuddle
49 Kind of hog
50 Moccasin
51 "Foucault's Pendulum" author
52 Unbent
53 Sad ER employee on d 3?
56 In a dour manner
57 Where Helen lived
58 Field event
59 Inquires
61 Mumblety-___ (jackknife game)
63 Mopped the deck
66 Envies
68 Pantyhose shade
70 Incendiarism
71 Man of Castilla
73 Imitate Gene Krupa
74 Biggest Little City
76 Soho subway
77 What rainbows are
79 Dot-com's address
81 Golf's Baker-Finch
82 Nils Diaz's org.
83 Neon or Neon-need

131 DIAMOND DEED by Pancho Harrison
The subtitle can be found at 43 Across.

ACROSS

1 Poetic foot
5 Treasury Dept. division
8 Crater edge
11 Mock words of understanding
15 Lady of the haus
16 José who wrote "Juiced"
18 Like morning meadows
19 Unaided
21 Creek at the Masters
22 Poppy derivative
23 Late 19th-century hairdo
24 Macadamize
25 Letterman's network
26 Aldrich Ames, for one
29 1847 Melville novel
31 Heloise offering
32 Text scanner: Abbr.
33 Haw's partner
34 Old film developer
36 Bellagio porters
38 Telecom giant
39 Corrida charger
42 ___ de toilette
43 SUBTITLE
48 Ballpark fig.
49 Scold
50 Meaningful nos. for Mensa
52 Vitamin C sources
56 Wear down
58 Trophy, sometimes
59 French friend
60 Bank regulating org.
62 Impertinent one
63 Count Fleet's feat
66 Nail, in a way
67 Freshwater duck
68 RC or Coke
69 Noxious effluvia
72 D.C. figures
73 Springfield simpleton
75 She sheep
76 Kittenish
77 They may be electric
78 Memo heading
79 Arlo, to Woody
80 Date
81 Where el sol rises

DOWN

1 "That being the case . . ."
2 "What ___-off!"
3 Stuffed-pasta dish
4 Bête noire
5 Arctic Blast maker
6 Cheery sound?
7 Big name in tools
8 Record voice-overs again
9 Arctic Ocean sight
10 Rocker's foe, in '60s London
11 "Kind of ___": Buckinghams
12 Rope puller's cry
13 Tonsor Todd
14 Frustrated utterances
17 Hog's honker
20 USMA grads
24 Bettor, at times
26 "That goes for me, too"
27 Syncretic
28 Logos, e.g.: Abbr.
29 "Birds ___ feather . . ."
30 Clothing consumer
31 Super Bowl intermission
35 Setting for many M*A*S*H scenes
36 Physics Nobelist Niels
37 Tampa Bay player, to fans
40 Eyes
41 Rural address abbr.
44 Golfer's need
45 Have a TV dinner, say
46 Elsa and Nala
47 Prefix with distant
51 Longtime Richard Petty sponsor
52 Sales slip: Abbr.
53 Thornton Wilder play
54 Circus pitchman
55 Mini-flute
57 One on the lam
60 Nashville legend Red
61 Animated miners
64 Obsolete
65 Director Polanski
66 Point
69 Thirty-two laps in the pool, say
70 Shed skin
71 "As I Lay Dying" father
72 Shar-___ (dog breed)
73 Some PCs
74 "A Boy Named ___"

ACROSS

1 Limited number
4 "C'mon!"
10 Green-light
14 Inca fortunes
16 Brownish oranges
17 Bogotá boy
18 Fail spectacularly
20 Lift a hot dog off the grill
21 Break down
22 Cyprus Museum locale
24 Picnic discard
25 Healthy breakfast food
28 Reagan proj.
30 Hussein's queen
31 Interjections from Rocky
32 Referee, before a kickoff
36 Puts in the hold
40 Like half a cyclical romance
41 Related maternally
43 ___ vous plaît
44 Overturns
46 Form a hypothesis
48 Emulated the Sprats
49 "Taxi" mechanic
51 Court arbiter
52 Former NYC restaurateur
54 1966 James Bond spoof
56 Upper-left button on a phone
58 One of Jacob's wives
59 Jennet
60 Cause of a bridge collapse, perhaps
64 Cadence count
66 Chopstick, e.g.
67 Rower
71 Helgenberger of "CSI"
72 Jason's quest
76 Prefix with business and chemical
77 Dispense, as justice
78 "The Witches" author
79 Lennon's "Beautiful Boy" subject
80 Size up

81 Part of AT&T

DOWN

1 Fictional circumnavigator
2 End of the old switch
3 Captain Queeg's creator
4 SoHo studio
5 Goethe's "The ___-King"
6 Part of a chorus line?
7 Theology inst.
8 Occupant of Friendship 7
9 Become bony
10 Down, at a diner
11 Place to post notices
12 "The Nanny Diaries" nanny
13 Exercise systems
15 Arrangement methods
16 Social rebuff
19 Wall St. deal
23 Make unavailable to the public
25 Dizzy Gillespie's genre
26 Lifeline, maybe
27 Fail to be
28 Beethoven's "Appassionata," e.g.
29 Something not to change in midstream?
30 51 past
32 Andean shrubs
33 Weaknesses
34 "Pygmalion" heroine
35 Overly enthusiastic
37 Father of Anubis
38 Mummifies
39 Cause of some skids

42 New driver, typically
45 Haunted house dangler
47 Recidivated
50 2-D measure
53 Rubbing out
55 Animal's gullet
57 Puzzlement
60 "Twenty Years After" author
61 French story
62 "Apostle of California"
63 Ice sheets
64 Knife handle
65 Web site
67 Load to bear
68 Packinghouse product
69 Aleve target
70 Liam Neeson film
73 ROTC grads
74 "Gidget" star
75 Goddess in a chariot

"ER" CANCELLED   by Billie Truitt
Don't stick an "N" in the name at 37 Down.

ACROSS

1 Action-movie scene
6 Collar location
10 Freak out
15 Women's group?
16 Amtrak's bullet train
18 Red, green, yellow, or white veggie
19 Late party at the neighbors' house?
21 He ran against Clinton and Bush
22 Bye-bye
23 "This is ___ for Superman!"
25 Purina competitor
26 Pumpernickel ingredient
27 Shortly, briefly
29 School of thought
30 She was Dear to many
33 Phony story?
36 Eastern way
37 Burst of laughter
38 Govt. securities
39 Chatty bird
41 Basketball commentator Elmore
43 Spin
44 Memoir of a lepidopterist?
49 Major League family name
50 Larry King's channel
51 Kitchen magnet?
53 Intermediary
56 Chocolate tidbit
58 Campfire seat
59 Laboratory funding?
63 "Anything ___?"
64 Young pond dweller
65 Very much
66 Common site of knee injuries
68 Had on
70 Baylor's home
71 Vacation souvenirs
75 Starr witness Linda
77 How to cook maize evenly?
79 Show opener
80 Key material
81 Half a record
82 Ghostly pale
83 Jump in the rink
84 Precipitous

DOWN

1 Small talk
2 Holy circle?
3 Alice's Restaurant customer
4 Lookout
5 Post of manners
6 Slangy refusals
7 Make a scene?
8 Academic showoff
9 Wood who played Frodo
10 Elephant gp.
11 Most draftable
12 Helicopter rescue, at times
13 Sweetie pie
14 Lays to rest
17 Win by ___
20 V-formation fliers
24 No longer ill
27 Cove
28 Multiplexes
30 Twenties dispenser
31 Indiana political name
32 U2 frontman
34 New Haven inst.
35 Use crayons
37 Jules Verne's Fogg
40 Come to
42 Big Apple initials
43 Confrontation
45 Anne ___ Lindbergh
46 Not sour
47 Kind of booth
48 Med. plans
52 Candle count
53 Dunk some Darjeeling
54 Improvements, of a kind
55 World's fastest biped
57 Secret supply
60 Orange box
61 Priam's wife
62 Bleach brand
63 Draw forth
67 Quest for a mate?
69 Fencing implement
71 E-mail sign-off
72 Took the subway
73 Nest site
74 Lose it
76 Slammer
78 U-turn from SSW

"HELLO, I MUST BE GOING" by Patrick Jordan
Alternate clue for 82 Across: Cinderella's horses, subsequently.

ACROSS

1 Zestfulness
6 Park pigeon's perch
12 Kid around with
16 Those who oppose
17 Riding on
18 "Render ___ Caesar . . ."
19 Greeting to a seismologist?
21 Rabin's predecessor
22 Dee who duetted with Elton
23 Asphalt ingredient
24 Branch out, as a business
26 Boom box feature
28 UPS delivery
31 Donnybrook
32 Ship captained by Vicente Pinzon
33 Earned an honorarium, perhaps
35 Fannie or Ginnie follower
38 Greeting to the Invisible Man?
43 Not suitable
45 Put into circulation
46 Laboratory vessel
47 In ___ (unmoved)
48 Certain stock buyer, briefly
50 Elevs.
51 15th New Testament book
52 Poker player's assertion
53 La Scala's location
55 Packers powerhouse Favre
56 Farewell to an escaped convict?
60 Pronoun for every second hurricane
61 Checked the flavor of
62 "In your dreams!"
64 1988 Summer Games site
67 Pension-paying govt. org.
68 Quarantine
72 Shares the value of
74 Porter or stout
75 "I see ___ moon rising . . .": CCR
76 Petunia, to Harry Potter
77 Farewell to a farmer?
82 Cinderella's horses, formerly
83 "Rambo" genre
84 Plymouth cofounder John
85 Barreled along
86 Bowling or boxing, but not hockey
87 Batik practitioners

DOWN

1 Stares stupidly
2 Like a square
3 Vampire vanquisher
4 Brownish orange hue
5 WWII spying org.
6 Reminiscent of a desert
7 Ski lift type
8 NASA affirmative
9 ___ chi (exercise program)
10 Cremains container
11 Cutting side
12 Cleared with a bound
13 Bryant's former teammate
14 Horror author R. L.
15 Teeming throng
20 Shorthand pro
25 Wolverine's squad
27 It's worn with a sporran
28 Some crockery
29 Flute-playing Hindu god
30 Entire range
34 Souvenir shirts
35 iPod output
36 Psychological inner self
37 "Weird" Al Yankovic parody
39 1960 Elvis musical
40 Analyzes, with "up"
41 "War of the Worlds" world
42 Inspire ecstasy in
44 Emphasized
48 Irving and Tan
49 Thigh-slapping jokes
54 Costar of Farr and Farrell
55 Vivacity, to Verdi
57 Corridor
58 Final part, redundantly
59 County bordering Suffolk
63 How the tone-deaf sing
64 Coal beds
65 Furnish gear for
66 Krugerrand's weight
69 Bear patiently
70 Whip wielder at a circus
71 Blissful spots
73 Fawn's father
74 Briefly, to a bard
78 Defrosting target
79 Env. enclosure
80 Lucy in "Shanghai Noon"
81 Diminutive degree

135 WHAT THE DOCTOR OUGHT TO ORDER   by Lucile Sloan
October 4, 1957 is the official date of 33 Across.

ACROSS

1 NASCAR sponsor
4 Make a law of
9 Has a long step
16 Hardly paleo
17 Alvin of Broadway
18 Charge for using
19 "Take Me as ___": Faith Hill
20 **Josh Billings quote: Part I**
22 Fall ___ grace
24 Orr teammate, familiarly
25 Cave effect
26 **Quote: Part II**
32 Take sustenance
33 It started with Sputnik
34 Bridge phrase
36 Went wild
38 About to receive
42 WW2 Axis leader
45 Parker in "Old Yeller"
46 Seat of Webster County, Ia.
48 Fla. neighbor
49 **Quote: Part III**
51 Dudgeon
52 Some bundles of joy
54 Phys. activity
55 Knocked off
56 "Woman Eating Oysters" artist
57 Mediterranean vessels
59 VW preceders
62 Taking a powder on the mound
66 "Freaks" director Browning
69 **Quote: Part IV**
71 "Bring ___" (2000 cheerleading movie)
73 Dobbin's restraint
74 Tropical starchy root
75 **Quote: Part V**
81 Part of a wd.
82 Tee transfers
83 Ex-New York governor
84 Games org.
85 Not mind
86 Work until smooth
87 Suffix with propyl or butyl

DOWN

1 Emulates a police dog
2 Begin to cry
3 Home of Cal Poly
4 Creepy crawler
5 "Forget it!"
6 Is for more than one?
7 Train section
8 Gershwin's "Of ___ Sing"
9 Gain admission quietly
10 "Receiving poorly," in CB talk
11 Untrustworthy one
12 "Woe ___!"
13 Low card
14 ___-Sketch
15 Not ___ (far from optimal)
21 "My Fair Lady" setting
23 Smaller than small
27 Granting grp.
28 Virile
29 White-tailed herons
30 Franklin, religiously
31 Bagnold and Blyton
35 Noted Tokyo-born singer
37 Milo of "Ulysses"
39 Bank-window initials
40 "The Lord of the Rings" creature
41 Walter ___ Hospital
42 Bandage in a way
43 Portrait studio ___ Mills
44 Jolts
46 Sans
47 Soprano Stratas
49 Quotable Yogi
50 Version's start
53 ___ au vin
55 "Ours ___ to reason why . . .": Tennyon
57 Desi's daughter
58 0, in soccer
60 Pilgrim's goal
61 Smaller than small
63 Rome's home, in France
64 "The Honeymooners" character
65 Aerospace measure
66 Marshmallowy
67 Comic actress Cheri
68 "Ice Age" birds
70 New York hoopster
72 Spanish kid
76 Corn throwaway
77 Cloister sister
78 Other side
79 Mia in "Pulp Fiction"
80 Signal at Sotheby's

ACROSS

1 Museum Folkwang locale
6 Put to the test
11 Place for a pumpkin
16 Gene Tierney classic film
17 More "compos mentis"
18 Plains tribe
19 Heavy-metal pioneers
21 Copier need
22 Weight Watchers member
23 Like Dracula
24 Shows
27 "The Dean Martin Show" dancers
30 Showered and shaved, say
32 ___ Marquette
33 Linda ___ (Supergirl)
34 Alternatively
35 All worked up
37 Big name in furniture rental
38 Dorothy Parker quality
39 Like Catherine Zeta-Jones
42 Apiece
44 Tennessee Williams classic
49 ___ the finish
50 Dapper
51 "Platoon" setting
53 Cathedral recess
56 Scrooge
58 Eight furlongs
59 ___ generis (unique)
60 Clinton cabinet member Federico
61 Speck
65 Party staple
68 Most warmed-up
69 Lexington's Rupp et al.
70 Brunch fare
72 Japanese cooking wine
73 Sure thing
78 "Silas Marner" author
79 Nighttime kitchen invader
80 Stevie Wonder's "My Cherie ___"
81 ___ College bigwigs
82 Cruel sorts
83 Animal hides

DOWN

1 "The Lord of the Rings" figure
2 Freelancer's enc.
3 ___ rosa
4 Learned
5 Compatriot
6 African menace
7 Hard to find
8 Prefix with red
9 Reef dweller
10 Like some wine
11 Soup, in a French restaurant
12 In a crowd of
13 Grapefruit cousin
14 Fan, at times
15 Can't be swayed, in jargon
20 "Aqua ___ Hunger Force"
23 Stinging colonist
24 All over again
25 Dig find
26 Haile Selassie disciple
28 Kick ___ storm
29 More than dislike
31 He ran away with the spoon
36 French wine region
37 Comedian Margaret
39 Hit the jackpot
40 Some paints
41 Barrio resident
43 Boo-hoo
45 Backgammon impossibility
46 Diamond cover
47 In reserve
48 Horseshoe ___
52 Track event
53 Red-faced
54 Childish
55 Sight of the Tunguska blast
57 ___ Paulo
58 Buy before a sale, e.g.
60 Double agents
62 Hebrew letters
63 Thespian's quest
64 Work boot feature
66 Negatively charged particle
67 Like some stock
71 Cheese nibblers
73 Ora ___ nobis
74 Cranberry area
75 Cambodia's Lon ___
76 Director's cry
77 Store posting: Abbr.

137 SHIFTY SLOGANS by Doug Peterson
19 Across won the Daytona 500 in 1991.

ACROSS

1 Goes for a dip
6 Some laptops
10 Togo, e.g.
16 River craft
17 Father of Ham
18 Meeting handout
19 Legendary NASCAR driver Ernie
20 "The River Sings" singer
21 Makes fine food?
22 Bisquick slogan?
25 Magnate Onassis
26 Calendar-watch abbr.
27 Beehive State resident
28 Bausch & Lomb slogan?
33 Glum
36 Associate of Freud
37 Right-hand page
38 Opposing force
40 Bellyached
42 Hardly a squeaker
44 Emmy winner Falco
45 AAA slogan?
49 Cocktail garnish
52 "Skedaddle!"
53 Prankster's cry
57 Madrid museum
59 Make fun of
62 Not at all
63 Droop
64 Formula 409 slogan?
67 Boca ___
69 Watch attachment
70 '50s political inits.
71 Speedo slogan?
76 Lemonlike fruit
77 Kind of vaccine
78 Sacred stand
80 Alternative to macaroni
81 Wile E. Coyote supplier
82 Unpleasant residue
83 End of a threat
84 Racing circuits
85 Elizabethan earl

DOWN

1 Chem. or phys.
2 Result of a hitch in the service?
3 Sweet-talk
4 Zoo barrier
5 In the mail
6 Mistakenly
7 Pep rally sight
8 BLT spread
9 ___-Pei dog
10 Hero of Super Bowl III
11 Work up
12 Sophomore's grade
13 Furious
14 German border river
15 Mil. landing site
23 Dee follower
24 Head for the hills
25 Steed with speed
29 Tested by lifting
30 BlackBerry rival
31 Cratchit's employer
32 "Believe ___ Not!"
34 Brest buddy
35 Turn blue
39 Trojan War counselor
41 Two-out plays: Abbr.
43 Dress (up)
46 Hallowed site
47 Lather
48 "The World of Suzie ___" (1960)
49 Vinyl spinners
50 401(k) cousin
51 "The Treachery of Images" painter
54 Italian table wines
55 Event with a friendly crowd
56 Leaves speechless
58 Auto extras
60 Freeway feature
61 Noggins
65 '80s White House nickname
66 Stat for a Mariner
68 Pop singer Lavigne
71 "New Look" designer
72 Stable newborn
73 Predator of the deep
74 Ming thing
75 Maladies
76 ___-Magnon
79 Stout of whodunits

138 BUSH THE LEADER by Billie Truitt
A puzzler's tribute to the 43rd president . . . or is it?

ACROSS

1 Costco competitor
5 Darrow defended him
11 Journalist Drudge
15 Neutral shade
16 Piano adjusters
17 Jiggly dessert
18 Range unit
19 One on the stump
20 Erie Canal city
21 Keep the ship's log?
24 Brain scan letters
25 "Not guilty," for one
26 Promotes
30 Centric starter
32 Body slam consequence?
36 Sniffs out
38 Fellow
39 Gluttony or pride
40 One of the five W's
41 Supermarket division
43 Rollercoaster segments
44 This life's struggles?
48 Root ___
49 Spread out
50 Juanita's year
51 Word to a family doctor
52 "Dig in!"
53 Winter sculpture
57 Sound of rustling gift paper?
62 Almanac tidbit
63 "Hogan's Heroes" character
64 Drying oven
66 Genealogy word
67 Prepare used clothes to drip dry?
72 Babble on
75 Dad's sister, affectionately
76 MP's quarry
77 Reno or Jackson
78 "Can't wait!" in Canterbury
79 On one's rocker?
80 Telescope sight
81 Canned heat
82 Units of work

DOWN

1 Kelp
2 Grow together
3 Man to marry
4 Bird feeder fat
5 Kitchen island seat
6 Homecoming times?
7 Even (with)
8 Anti-fur gp.
9 Cupid's counterpart
10 Ukr. and Est., once
11 Shooting star
12 Will Smith title role
13 Convalescent's need
14 Grind ___ halt
17 "A ___ Wine, a Loaf . . .": Khayyám
22 Ages
23 Blood-typing letters
27 Rug fiber
28 "Fun, Fun, Fun" car
29 Payroll IDs
31 More up-to-date
33 Shake up
34 Like an easy job
35 MacLachlan of "Desperate Housewives"
37 Little ones
41 Company with a spokesduck
42 McGregor in "Stormbreaker"
43 Three, perhaps
44 "___ the Champions": Queen
45 Post-injury program
46 Diner sign
47 Sworn in
48 Cry like a baby
53 Grand Central, for one
54 Fabled racehorse
55 Everlasting
56 1956 Kentucky Derby winner
58 Tankard metal
59 Editor's mark
60 Yes, to Yvette
61 Computer network device
65 Shorthand expert
68 Constant carpers
69 Mex. neighbor
70 Treater's phrase
71 Alleviate
72 Sleepover attire, briefly
73 2008 Chinese calendar icon
74 Santa in California

139 SOPHISTICATED LADY by Norman S. Wizer
A felicitous title and the name of a classic Rosemary Clooney recording.

ACROSS

1 Repository
6 Liturgical vestments
10 Sinbad's land
16 Ice house
17 12/26 event
18 They're made at bars
19 Rosemary sang with his band
21 Quartet + trio
22 Memorabilia
23 Went through channels?
25 Fontaine offering
26 Marvin and Merriweather
28 Cinerary vessel
29 It's found on the streets
33 1951 Rosemary Clooney hit
37 ___ corpus
40 Mushroom
41 Deal maker
42 The footlights
43 Source of suds
46 1954 Rosemary Clooney hit
49 1952 Rosemary Clooney hit
52 Clio winners
53 Poke
55 Kind of symmetry
56 Puts down
58 Idle
59 1954 Rosemary Clooney film
64 Put another way
65 New Zealand bird
66 Beat down
70 Trip of sorts
71 Tickle
75 Thailand language
76 Rain cloud
80 1954 Rosemary Clooney film
82 It's between the pages
83 Pundit
84 Spine-tingling
85 Set
86 Got with difficulty
87 Break in

DOWN

1 Life-giving
2 Time past, time past
3 Radii companions
4 She played Mrs. Charles
5 Blue-ribbon
6 Free from doubt
7 Ricky Martin's music
8 Political group
9 Withered
10 Jenny may be one
11 Charlotte of "Diff'rent Strokes"
12 Gran Paradiso, e.g.
13 Bayou boat
14 Prototypes
15 Perceptive
20 Reuners
24 Scratch up
27 Hound's clue
30 Seductive singer: Var.
31 21st Greek letter
32 In ___ signo vinces
34 Inauguration Day vow
35 Washington slugger
36 Banded quartz
37 Silly fence?
38 Kept in the cellar, perhaps
39 Turkish governors
42 Meal with matzoh
43 Destiny's Child, e.g.
44 Word of consolation
45 Gomer of Mayberry
47 Put on the books
48 Hied
50 Computer input
51 Have being
54 E-commerce giant
56 NFL passing stat
57 "Golden Girl" Arthur
58 Normandy beach
59 Monkey ___
60 Flight to freedom
61 Chemical "twin"
62 Just a little bit
63 Dressed
67 On the qui vive
68 Victor ___ Hugo
69 Puzzling problem
72 Enya's language
73 News source, at times
74 Home of Keebler elves
77 Like Peck's boy
78 Put into practice
79 Change on the Ginza
81 Yellow Monopoly bill

140 IT MARCHES ON by Jinx Davidson
40 Across ranks behind Great Britain and Iceland in size.

ACROSS

1 Backslide
6 Single-minded theorizer
12 Glen Gray's Casa ___ Orchestra
16 Lands in the ocean
17 Kansas city suburb
18 "About" preceders in charges
19 Bellyaches
20 Infection result, perhaps
21 Cold pack
22 Stall
23 "In other words . . ."
25 More elliptical, in a way
27 Shucker's unit
28 Bracket type
29 Old can material
30 Check number
33 Sajak or Trebek
35 Willy of "Death of a Salesman"
38 Morales in movies
39 LDS-related campus
40 Europe's 3rd-largest island
42 Swing site
44 Girl from 40 Across
48 Toy ball brand
49 Goad, with "on"
51 Was idle
52 Jean-Claude Van Damme film
53 De follower?
54 Flying formations
56 Herring delicacy
58 Poetic tribute
60 Subsequently
62 Evil one
63 Greeting
66 Laceration
67 Brother's title
68 Court winner
69 Env. content
71 Ration out
76 "It's been a pleasure"
80 Slip ___ (blunder)
81 Stare open-mouthed
82 Philippine province
83 Hard wear?

84 Bank claim
85 "Mad" man
86 Fred's familial partner
87 Muffs
88 Manages
89 Loan security

DOWN

1 Trunk attachments
2 "Modern Man in Search of ___": Jung
3 Costa del Sol feature
4 Overly nostalgic sort
5 Snaky shape
6 Israeli leader Dayan
7 Mrs. ___ cow
8 "I'm taking a siesta!"
9 "___ small world!"
10 Eye shadow?
11 Seed coat
12 Gray wolf
13 "Hold on!"
14 Spirit
15 Diamond-shaped pattern
23 Take the cake
24 Junior's son
26 "Dennis the Menace" girl
31 Grab a bite
32 Goes on TV
34 Storage units
35 Swimmer Jeremy
36 Three-layer treat
37 Raconteur Griffin
38 Cusp
39 Eliza follower?
41 Torino Olympic mascot of 2006
43 Toward the rising sun
45 Zoning unit
46 By and by
47 Zoomed

50 Kind of therapy
55 Neptune's realm
57 Bushy do
59 Blockhead
61 Roentgenologist's place
63 Quibble
64 Patisserie product
65 Good rebounder, usually
66 "The Rose of ___"
67 Winter health concern
70 Self-contained entity
72 Hardly rational
73 Zeniths
74 "A Confederacy of Dunces" author
75 "Snowy" bird
77 Retreats
78 "Stop the clock"
79 Rice and Robbins
83 Miami Heat home

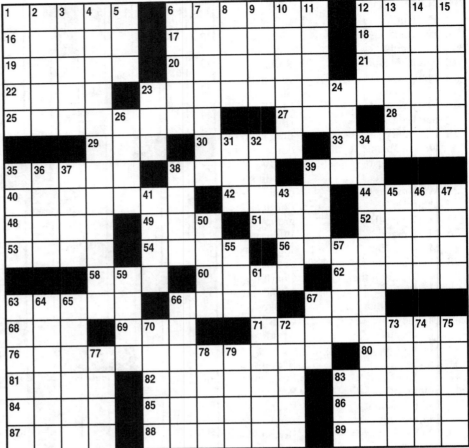

PROMPT JUDGMENT by Patrick Jordan

Lon Chaney, Jr., and Benicio del Toro have both played 24 Across.

ACROSS

1 Passages between peninsulas
7 Pick up vibes about
12 Cello's range
16 Lebanese University site
17 Fusion weapon, for short
18 Diva's rendition
19 **Quip by E.V. Lucas: Part 1**
21 Adept at deception
22 Hydropathic facility
23 Asparagus shoot
24 Hairy howler of horror
26 Having a screw loose
28 Texas Revolution fort
29 Pas' partners
32 Nebr. neighbor
33 Throw off one's trail
36 **Quip: Part 2**
39 Mme., in Mazatlán
42 Performs adequately
43 Grinner's emotion
44 "Get Smart" enemy org.
45 Welcome
46 "Seventh heaven"
48 Signs of bad shock absorbers
49 Bridge builder James
50 Strategist's concoction
51 Gesture to a general
52 "Reach for the ___!" ("Stick 'em up!")
53 **Quip: Part 3**
56 Frugal shopper's concern
57 UAE member?
58 Pegs, briefly
59 Echo-testing shout, often
62 Stropped item
64 Globe girder

67 Bombastic outbursts
69 Big bankroll
72 Patty or Selma, to Bart
73 **Quip: Part 4**
76 Popular fashion
77 Without letup
78 Tick away
79 "Mush!" yeller's vehicle
80 "Clash by Night" playwright
81 IOU writer

DOWN

1 Curve-billed wader
2 Twice-monthly tide
3 Succotash bean
4 Memorable span
5 Soaking spots
6 Retreat a little
7 Massage technique
8 "The Great Movies" author Roger
9 Guy Fawkes Day mo.
10 Small fishing duck
11 Spain's most voluminous river
12 Throw for a loop
13 Coffee shop lure
14 Early riser's hr.
15 Refuse
20 Wasn't quite perpendicular
25 ___-in-waiting
27 Cheerleader's repertoire
29 Tiny buzzers
30 Greenland wear
31 Bullet train adjective
32 Gordian or granny, e.g.
34 Contends (for)
35 Absorbed the cost of
37 Applications
38 Not getting any younger
39 Slender hunting dog
40 Broke down
41 Size up
44 Pop-flavoring nut
46 International alliance
47 "Today" talker Matt
48 Door frame upright
50 Upsilon follower
51 Gave quite a turn to
53 Sulky puller's pace
54 Duffer's obstacles
55 "The Gift of the Magi" device
56 Like an armadillo
59 Gets wind of
60 Sharing a value
61 Fencing move
63 "You ___ serious?" ("Is this a joke?")
65 Melville book set in Tahiti
66 Rip apart
68 Brogue's bottom
69 Reacted to a tearjerker
70 "Not to mention . . ."
71 One who tints togs
74 Skein formation
75 Slap the cuffs on

ACROSS

1 Nae sayer
5 Sprints toward
11 Blondie drummer Burke
15 Name on an IRA
16 Like some bonds
17 University of Hawaii locale
18 Title by 78 Across/SUBTITLE
20 Words heard by mice
21 Bless with oil
22 "Excuse me . . ."
23 Gift for Rapunzel
24 Checkbook record
26 It's abuzz with activity
28 Level
31 Double-wide pram*
36 Knock, slangily
37 Pricey
38 Bonn article
39 Ketel ____ vodka
40 Shake hands on
42 Monster's loch
45 Italian soprano Renata
47 30, at times*
50 World Cup chant
51 "Right!"
52 Defeat Federer in the first round
54 Sun god
55 Constellation near Scorpius
57 "Mama" Elliot
59 Mozart's gift
60 Marathon ender*
64 Queue after Q
65 Its capital is Pristina
66 Mariposa lily variety
68 Low point
71 Bullfrog genus
73 Throat soother
77 Plath's "Tale of ____"
78 Russian physician/playwright
80 A word from Mork
81 Foster's brown-haired girl
82 "____ Rock": Simon & Garfunkel
83 Tulip supporter
84 Skillful
85 Richie Rich's collar

DOWN

1 Mex. miss
2 Joe McCarthy's counsel Roy
3 Other, in Cancun
4 Belief in God
5 Bollywood star Aishwarya
6 Nocturnal bear
7 Detroit on Broadway
8 Leaves Earl Grey in hot water
9 It'll eat you out of house and home
10 Takes too much
11 Classic supermodel Tiegs
12 Stead
13 Antlered critters
14 Slam dance
16 Knowing
19 Med. specialty
23 Tracheal branch
25 Swahili honorific
27 Come into being
28 Christian denom.
29 Poker variety
30 Haifa native
32 "Your honor, ____ my case . . ."
33 Egyptian water lilies
34 Request
35 ____ Speedwagon
37 Economics measure
41 Mik Kaminski's group
43 Boston Pops sect.
44 Took a bit of needling
46 Alley in the comics
48 Parisian papas
49 Gets better
50 East of Germany
53 Capote, to friends
56 Decorated
58 Boil over with anger
61 Downwardly mobile sort
62 Incarnation
63 Words of protest
64 Yankee Stadium newbie
67 Upper-level coll. entry test
68 Bobbsey and Robertson
69 Rat-____
70 Novel set in the year 10,991
72 Years in old Rome
74 Palaver
75 Jacob Epstein's "Ecce ____"
76 "Mrs. Bridge" author Connell
78 Classic Steely Dan album
79 Op. ____

143 WEATHER OR NOT   by Arlan and Linda Bushman
Santa's throwing the party at 19 Across.

ACROSS

1 Ridiculous
7 Brace (oneself)
11 Recklessness
16 Oil-rich sultanate
17 Son of Seth
18 Steer clear of
19 North Pole party?
21 Patches
22 Headstrong
23 Dance partner
24 Record label letters
26 Journey of 2009?
27 Kind of shot
28 Playwright Shepard
31 Time span
34 Flat cause
37 Jungle hacker
39 Solon consideration
40 Snaps
41 Prison in 1971 headlines
42 ___ around
44 Ways
45 Finding time to relax, e.g.?
48 Drive (out)
51 Meal makings
52 Beguile
56 Broadway musical
57 Antediluvian
58 Nitty-gritty
59 Fickle demeanor?
63 Andean honchos
64 Stake
65 Miniature
66 Winter Palace occupant
68 Minn. neighbor
69 Souter attire
71 Superficial
74 Excellent
76 Frosty's concern?
79 Stand-up's delivery
80 On the house
81 Singly
82 Hound's clue
83 Popular sneakers
84 Packed compactly together

DOWN

1 Mideast garment
2 Cold call?
3 To the point
4 Golden Rule word
5 This pulls a bit
6 Pronouncements
7 Italian treat
8 Lined up
9 Like some cheeks
10 Mar. event
11 Celebrated
12 Baker
13 Best personal asset
14 Maximum
15 Draper's meas.
20 Scorched, in Montreal
23 Oodles
24 Austen classic
25 Defensive feature
27 Swiss capital
29 Keystone's place
30 Snafu
32 Copse
33 "Men in Trees" star
35 Court responses
36 Austere
38 ___ chi
42 Wesley Snipes vampire flick
43 Newt, once
44 Sophia Loren hubby Carlo
46 Sucker, informally
47 Peg
48 Rebuff
49 Colliery
50 Picketing
53 Carom
54 Philosopher Watts
55 "Hey!"
57 Orchestral tuner
58 No laughing matter
60 Most favorably
61 Paid the penalty
62 Matters for discussion
67 Put on again
70 Auspice
71 Close attention
72 Model
73 "How sweet ___!"
74 REM-time wear
75 "Arabian Nights" flier
76 RMN rival
77 Sharapova coup
78 Combine

ACROSS

1. New Zealand aborigine
6. Toll area
11. Hacienda brick
16. Out of this world?
17. Big name in morning TV
18. Steakhouse order
19. Worked on pumps
20. Pizza places
21. Minimum
22. **Start of a definition of "Dijon vu"**
25. Blue
26. Towhead
27. Satisfied the munchies
28. Chevy Colorado predecessor
29. Fermi's study
32. Scoutmasters, mostly
36. Small swallow
38. The time of your life
40. WWW addresses
42. Flight formation
43. Driver's target
45. Leather-___ (very loud)
47. Nut-brown quaff
48. **Middle of definition**
52. Jackie's 1968 husband
53. Disclaimer
54. "The Eve of St. Agnes" writer
55. The big house
56. Put in one's two cents?
57. Camel dropping
60. Is, for two
61. Competitive plus
63. Cub Scout groups
65. Point to the left?
67. Simile words
69. "Magic Man" group
71. Batter's success
74. **End of definition**
80. Dreadlocked dude
81. Hopping mad
82. Heathen
83. Phenol compound
84. In a spin
85. Emulate Cicero
86. In need of cash
87. Intrinsically
88. Triple trio

DOWN

1. Brig twosome
2. Hilo hello
3. Drunk as a skunk
4. Boating hazard
5. Owing
6. Stretch out
7. "The Stepford Wives" author
8. It may be hidden
9. Energy
10. Kind of mgr.
11. Equivalent of G sharp
12. Reduced the fare
13. Oil of crosswords
14. "You'd ___ Nice to Come Home To"
15. Rebuke from Caesar
23. Where Zeno taught
24. Best Picture of 1948
28. Noted Graf
30. Arctic plain
31. Bacchanalia
33. Incarnation in human form
34. Strike out
35. Crop starters
36. Fearful
37. "The Legend of Sleepy Hollow" author
39. "Pipers piping" number
41. Mt. Rushmore loc.
43. Condition
44. Role for Radner
46. Persian Gulf fed.
49. Lugosi portrayer
50. Bar mitzvah, e.g.
51. Parliament prize
58. Wrap with bandages
59. Basil, for one
62. Egg-roll time
64. Lad
66. Treat badly
68. Nobody's fool
70. Empire State Indians
71. "Crocodile Dundee" star
72. Hopping mad
73. Article of faith
74. Uno + dos
75. Diner specialty
76. :, in analogies
77. Cuff
78. Pirelli product
79. Las Vegas game

145 SIX THAT SOUND THE SAME by Regimen L. Evers
34 Across enrolled at Stanford in the fall of 2007.

ACROSS

1 Goombah
4 Act inconspicuously
10 Tell to sit a spell
15 "Don't have ___, man!"
17 White fur
18 Nebraska Indian
19 Ride rider's shout
21 Hidden mikes
22 Clinton's 1993 inauguration started one
23 City southwest of Padua
25 Take without asking
26 Ohio college
29 Where Wales is
31 Center in central Florida
34 Honolulu-born golfer
38 Movie cowboy Lash
39 Cornrow
40 German industrial center
41 Free-swinging Ruben
43 Figure of speech
45 "___ Tu" (1974 hit)
46 Developing
49 Habit
53 Two twelfths
54 Coming from both sides
56 Word before box
60 Bolt to get hitched
63 Horoscope writer Sydney
64 Xbox 360 rival
66 Hiding hiker of kiddie lit
67 Old convertible name
68 Over
70 "___ take arms against . . .": Shak.
71 Blurt out
75 Picks via polls
79 Herald's locale
81 Yes to a Frenchman
84 Spaniard's "these"
85 Soda jerks hand them out
86 Camping equipment
87 Pad user
88 Walk like a baby
89 Wave carrier

DOWN

1 One of 16 in chess
2 Workout consequence, maybe
3 Movie mogul Marcus
4 "The Merry Widow" composer
5 George's lyrical brother
6 CPR user, sometimes
7 It's insurable
8 It's carried on the shoulders
9 Shoved off
10 Actress Clara
11 Ellis Island visitors
12 Gets smaller
13 Inferior product
14 Fading star
16 Two and three a.m., say
20 Word processor user
24 Sniggler's catch
27 Roadie's burden
28 Measure of thickness
30 Peter Fonda's favorite role
31 Threat ender
32 Eyes or ears
33 Tribe of Canada
35 Purina product
36 Put in a position?
37 Captain Hook's alma mater
42 Singer DiFranco
44 Quart divs.
47 Cut from the payroll
48 Normandy battleground of '44
49 Arrivers' comment
50 Dental school exam?
51 No jock
52 Ring rampager
53 Dump closure?
55 "His" and "Hers" items
56 Workers make them
57 Pepys, for one
58 Tuition classification
59 Footstool
61 Dessert wedge
62 Nietzsche article
65 San Francisco hill
69 Clueless
72 Clueless
73 One with a painted body
74 Oriole or cardinal
76 2.0 grades
77 Something to whistle
78 Madrid Mlle.
80 Equi- relative
82 "Cracked" competitor
83 Mouse catcher

146 THERE'S MONEY IN IT by Jay Sullivan
60 Across is a popular dance in Lafayette, Louisiana.

ACROSS

1 Jeanne d'Arc, par exemple
7 S&L offering
11 Pleased as punch
15 NAFTA component
16 Made the cut
17 A Golden Girl
18 What banks pay in Romania?
20 Think piece
21 Cut down to size
22 Sun star
23 Inexpensive Delhi footwear?
29 Big tops
30 PC program extension
31 Helping that doesn't help the waist
36 Dredge up
38 Soliloquize
39 Snake alarm
40 The eyes have it
44 Sought a second term
45 Net earnings, in Nogales?
49 Volunteer's response
51 Gave the slip
52 Zsa Zsa's sister
55 In stereo
57 First-class sailor
60 Cajun jig
61 Disney picture
64 Monk's music
65 Polish gambler's preference?
68 Shylock's trade
72 Geronimo, for one
73 "Don't think so!"
74 Saudi currency venture?
80 Course elective
81 Capital of central Asia
82 Indelicate
83 Care for
84 Chicano bears
85 At first, perhaps

DOWN

1 Mineo of the movies
2 Leader of the pack
3 Post-op stop
4 Discouraging words
5 Least original
6 Ferber and Everage
7 One of the Pleiades
8 Pipsqueak
9 Some TV's
10 Summer Mass. hours
11 Put on a happy face
12 Pocket full of gold
13 Gone fishing, perhaps
14 Howie Mandel offering
16 Coil
19 Floor decor
22 Annual awards event
23 Household cleaners
24 Sci-fi craft
25 Undefiled
26 It's quite a stretch
27 Beat the heat?
28 No longer in the U.S. Army
32 Bread spread
33 Old salt
34 Small inheritance
35 AARP member
37 Sugar suffix
38 Not worth ___ cent
41 Bargain-basement
42 Veg out
43 It'll never fly
46 Unfortunately
47 Accident-prone
48 Mad men, briefly
49 Resident of the former Biafra
50 Patriots' victory
53 Wind instrument
54 Mound builders
56 Mom or pop
58 Tier
59 Yellowfin tuna
61 "Othello" setting
62 Net receipts
63 Like doilies
66 Karate-like exercise program
67 New Mexico canyon
68 Military outfit
69 In need of liniment
70 Well-versed in
71 Tear up
74 WBC result
75 Suffers from
76 Small serving
77 Thing of the past
78 Dolt
79 Rebel leader

147 CLUES TO AMUSE by Matt Ginsberg
The answer to 8 Down is not SHOE SOLE.

ACROSS

1 High points of a Swiss vacation
5 Bean head
9 Fare trade
16 Limited support
17 Actress Spelling
18 Medium settings
19 Some say it's bliss
21 Payers of flat fees
22 Trend follower
23 What this is
25 Modern "art"
26 Abridge too far?
27 Major 2001 bankruptcy
28 Page in "Juno"
30 "Night at the ___" (2006)
32 "XXX" org.
33 Gets back to business
37 Maegashira's sport
39 A bit of chemistry
43 Mohair
44 Words after "we meet"
46 Private address?
47 Where "stop" is a period
49 Pointless
51 Cockney's main Web page
52 Make an outstanding design
54 Alarmist
55 Exchange letters
57 Extra-wide width
58 Not right at all?
59 Singing the blues
61 "Key Largo" star
63 Black item
66 Family heads
67 Blast from the past
72 Rebel with a cause
73 Lock on a key
75 Dynamic beginning
76 Acted the ham
78 Entrance fee
80 Acknowledgment of error
81 Casual evening
82 French bean?
83 Bill sponsor
84 Hellenic letters
85 Flanders river

DOWN

1 Bring up the rear
2 Head producer
3 Chris craft
4 Change channels
5 "M*A*S*H" character?
6 Alternative to smoking
7 Like federal tax laws
8 Cobbler's bottom
9 Emoticon "eyes"
10 Man of war
11 The back of the choir
12 Pops in the fridge
13 Intestinal
14 "Nothing runs like a ___"
15 Düsseldorf neighbor
20 Come again
24 Rhea Silvia's son
27 Soup starter
29 "___ note to follow sew . . ."
31 Gun shy
32 Breather
33 Sing at Sing Sing
34 Other side
35 Checks figures
36 "Ulalume" poet
38 Dog's best friend
40 Chair person
41 Basso's house
42 Shooter's target
44 Examples of low life
45 Down time?
48 Copper head
50 Peabody in "Midnight"
53 Water wings?
56 Brooklyn follower
58 Head for Vegas
60 Dined downtown
62 Redact jointly
63 Country squares
64 Lion's amount
65 Town car
66 Product of the press
68 Peevish
69 Spooky sounding tribe
70 Struck from the Bible
71 Skin bracer
74 Emperor that fiddled around
75 Binders
77 "Love ___ Simple Thing"
79 Training org.

19 Across are enshrined in the National Aviation Hall of Fame in Dayton.

ACROSS

1 Comparable (to)
5 Exalted
12 CCCP
16 Plumb crazy
17 Verona's "Piazza dei ___"
18 "Fly's in the buttermilk, ___ . . ."
19 They made history on 12/17/1903
22 Blast from the past
23 Live and breathe
24 S, to a pilot
25 Luxurious resorts
28 Tolkien beast
30 More like the Kalahari
31 "Coming of age" ceremony
36 Hilary Duff song
37 Disney deer
38 Stern's opposite
39 Glasgow gal
41 Minnesota Fats feat
43 Block, in a way
46 Kon-Tiki Museum site
50 Messy
52 Not worth a ___
53 Buckle
55 Crystal ball user
56 Turns inside out
59 Knox and Courage
60 Fill to excess
62 Mao's successor
64 Sensitive subject, to some
65 John ___ Passos
68 Precisely punctual
72 Dispatch boat
74 Berne's river
75 "Take ___!"
76 Derelict
78 Acapulco aunt
80 Give a shave forward
84 Pen one to Penn. Ave
88 Groundless
89 Howard Hughes owned one
90 Joie de vivre
91 Refusals
92 Moves closer to the aisle
93 Stiff hair

DOWN

1 Voice below soprano
2 Milwaukee Bucks owner Herb
3 Put away, as a game
4 Not at all
5 Letter after chi
6 18-wheeler
7 Turkish honorific
8 Emcee lines
9 Gets on the wagon (with "up")
10 Be mistaken
11 "Vaya Con ___"
12 "My Boo" singer
13 Mideast prince
14 Reddish brown
15 Prayer beads
20 In the La-Z-Boy
21 Surfers concerns
26 Back of the boat
27 Design detail
29 Rodeo ropee
31 Romulus slew him
32 Cockamamie
33 Small sample
34 Make smile
35 Whaler's spear
40 Ho-hum
42 Churchill and McCartney
44 Anderson's "High ___"
45 Best
47 Fine fiddle
48 Send packing
49 Beginning
51 Himalayan bigfoot
54 Hamid Karzai, for one
57 Lyra's brightest star
58 Dispatched
61 Cropped up
63 Ultimate degree
65 "Origin of Species" author
66 Exaggerate
67 Neat as a pin, for one
69 Sour sorts
70 Diamond feat
71 Chopin pieces
73 Positions
77 One doesn't rate well
79 Met solo
81 Remove from a manuscript
82 No-see-um
83 Peak near Taormina
85 Shake a leg
86 Med. specialty
87 Parisian possessive

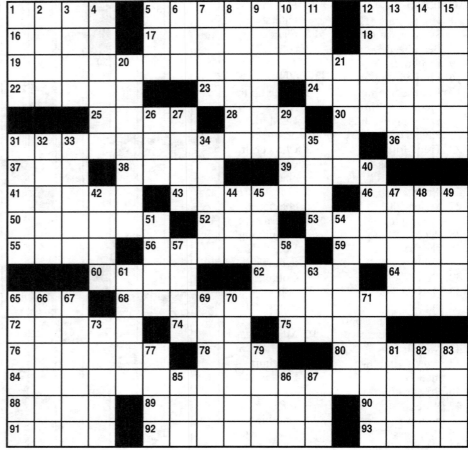

149 ADDING INSULT TO . . . by O. C. Hayes
This puzzle may suffer from a lack of respect.

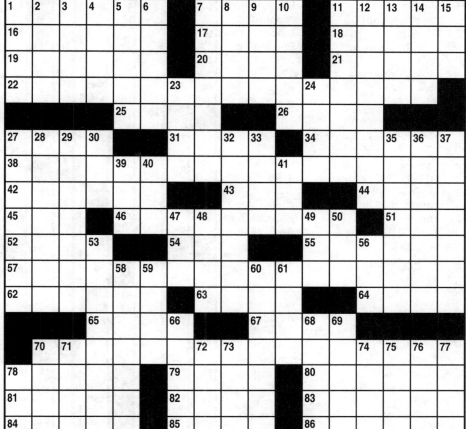

ACROSS

1 Light type
7 American Samoa, e.g.: Abbr.
11 Nav. officers
16 Part of a pizza ad, often
17 Hirsute biblical twin
18 Endangered gazelle
19 NASCAR family
20 Whitey Ford's pitching coach
21 Use an atomizer
22 Lowering the price of ewes?
25 Adult pup
26 Kibbutz grandpa
27 Egyptian deity
31 Movers' inventory
34 ELO album
38 Showcase next to a book of regulations?
42 Clever
43 Day-___ paint
44 Domesticated
45 Foreman KO'er
46 Divided into segments
51 Braz. neighbor
52 Bowflex features
54 Home-financing org.
55 Jot in a log
57 Eras in which we didn't get what we wanted?
62 Recreational vehicle
63 Leo component
64 Scrimmage wear
65 Perceived
67 Deuces
70 Cause the loss of safely shipped parcels?
78 Scouting group
79 Switch tail?
80 Eats into
81 Render nugatory
82 12 Down is one
83 "Tear down this wall" speaker
84 Illegal take
85 Brit. gallantry awards
86 Convictions

DOWN

1 Gulf war missile
2 Novelist Morrison
3 Filmmaker Meyer
4 Cartel founded in 1960
5 1963 U.S. Open winner
6 Follow
7 Research site
8 Mr. Morales
9 Precipitate
10 Ladder features
11 Where imbibing guests pay
12 Planters pitchman
13 Serious
14 "___ the Wild Wind" (DeMille movie)
15 Designing
23 Dark shade
24 Pre-Windsor name
27 Items checked at the door
28 Kind of steak
29 Mom's argument ender
30 Coppertone no.
32 Frank Gifford was one
33 Capital of Manche
35 Where Helen Keller grew up
36 Took down a notch
37 Unavailing
39 Mil. titles
40 Popeye's "Positively!"
41 "Angel"
47 Exec who deals with money
48 None of that?
49 Tackle's teammate
50 Initial follower
53 Turns in
56 Pointer
58 Dazzling display
59 Feather: Prefix
60 Body art
61 Port city or the lake it's on
66 Exercise
68 Make, as an effort
69 Jag
70 Fleming villain
71 Prefix for sphere
72 Piccadilly statue
73 Unworkable
74 Certain horse
75 Barely better
76 Musical chairs goal
77 Payroll IDs
78 Hunter of film and song

150 ABBEY ROAD REUNION   by Barry C. Silk
A reunion held within the circles in the squares.

ACROSS
1 Loosened (up)
7 Classify
13 Lisa Simpson, to Bart
16 Words after "because"
17 Taser, e.g.
18 It's used at Gallaudet U.
19 Colorful testudinate
21 Second Amendment advocacy gp.
22 "Show Boat" author Ferber
23 Ranked player
24 August 15, 1945
26 Timid type
31 Toward the stern
33 Justice Dept. worker
34 USN clerk: Abbr.
35 Tie with a clasp
36 Salvation Army founder
38 Injured party
41 Its symbol is Sn
42 Beige
43 Barbara of "Mission: Impossible"
45 Pod opening?
47 Viper on the Gadsden flag
53 State confidently
54 Bundles of dough
55 Took advantage of
56 11th-century date
59 "Panther in the Basement" novelist
61 Worked at a nabe
62 Zwei halved
64 Cyclone center
65 Litigator's org.
67 Globetrotter Nellie
68 Ottawa official
73 Billy Joel's "The Downeaster ___"
74 Smashnova of tennis
75 Lays down the lawn
78 Cigarette substance
79 Krispy Kreme offering
84 Mil. academy
85 Like farmland
86 Attached, in a way
87 Once named
88 Mooring rope
89 Emphasize

DOWN
1 Paper towel, e.g.
2 "It's ___ state of affairs!"
3 Cause for a delay in play
4 Avian chatterbox
5 Ballpark fig.
6 Accomplishes the task
7 Pontiac SUV
8 Jordanian's neighbor
9 Apr. season
10 Settle on
11 Divinity school subject: Abbr.
12 Rome's Fontana di ___
13 1993 baseball film (with "The")
14 Sabra
15 Mercury astronaut Deke
20 Door ding
25 Responsibility
27 Root word?
28 First U.S. capital
29 Age
30 Articulates
31 Prep a perp
32 Central points
37 Horn of plenty?
38 Itinerary word
39 Divided
40 Steele and Hood: Abbr.
43 City on the Weser
44 Dry gulch
46 Daunting burden
48 "The Loco-Motion" singer Little ___
49 Looney Tunes devil, for short
50 Fair-haired lass
51 Ship stabilizer
52 Watery swirl
56 Payload measure
57 Encroach on
58 4, to 1/4
60 Sun. address
61 Bygone Mideast fed.
63 Mae West play
65 Part of A.D.
66 Humdingers
69 Indian prince
70 Crystal of country music
71 Rear-___
72 Peter of Peter and Gordon
76 Pairs
77 CSX stops: Abbr.
80 Steve Carlton's was 3.22
81 Murphy's is well-known
82 Abbr. on a barbell
83 "Vamoose!"

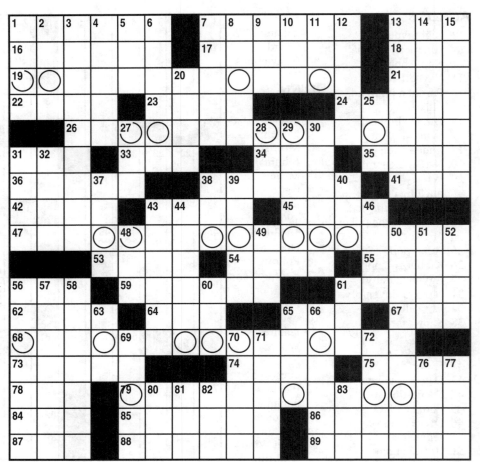

ACROSS

1 Nose or numeral type
6 Environmentalist Leopold
10 Eagles coach Andy
14 Corneille drama (with "Le")
17 Build up
18 Cervine creature
19 "All ___": Sinatra
20 Hwy.
21 SET
23 "... to buy ___ pig"
24 Deadly snake
25 Unique person
26 Play
27 SET
29 Church superstructure
31 College, e.g.
33 Basel river
34 Ages
35 SET
38 Polite addresses
39 Evil Disney lion
41 Canadian peninsula
42 Shoppers' cartways
43 Cause to converge
45 NFL linemen
46 Richard Pryor's daughter
48 Over, to Otto
49 Declarations
52 "Destry Rides Again" heroine
57 Member of a New York tribe
59 Time period
60 Boring
61 Junk yard, to some
62 Black sheep
64 Mammoth
65 Leopold's codefendant
67 Through-the-teeth utterance
68 Petty
69 Clown McDonald
73 Comparable to a beet
76 Peyton Manning, for one
77 Académie
78 SET
80 N.T. book
83 Glacial pinnacle
84 TV radio station
85 To ___ (somewhat)
87 SET
89 Yucca relative
92 Mountain in Thessaly
93 Purina brand
94 1963 role for Shirley
95 SET
97 To hear: Span.
98 Medical suffix
99 Speaker in the field
100 "Doctor Zhivago" producer
101 Make lace
102 The "N" of Rock's CSNY
103 Clockmaker Thomas
104 Mork, by birth

DOWN

1 Rest
2 Tooth: Comb. form
3 SET
4 Lit
5 Gotham paper, initially
6 Flips over
7 She played Glinda in "The Wiz"
8 Regard
9 Decrees
10 Tesla model
11 Devitalized
12 Muslim leader
13 SET
14 Skull-related
15 "My treat!"
16 Bring down
22 Goof-off
28 Words of discovery
30 Electronic organizers
32 Pile
36 "Taxi" driver's nickname
37 Wind-sprint
40 Preserves
42 Buenos ___
43 A hothead has a short one
44 Take orders from
45 Indian royal
47 Out to get
49 Stringed instrument of India
50 Treasure from the Atocha shipwreck
51 Like paint applied too thickly
53 Nothing: Lat.
54 SET
55 Hurricane of 1989
56 River of France and Belgium
58 SET
63 Pakistan's official language
66 Strong adverse reaction
68 Style
69 Do another take of
70 South Pacific island group
71 Mathematician Wiener
72 Kyrgyzstan range
74 NYSE unit
75 Meals
76 Gave up
78 Hindu mystics
79 Extravagant
81 Former Spanish currency
82 Turn toward the port
86 Dig
88 Latin for "bear"
90 Environmentalist Al
91 Landed
96 NYSE event

152 "NOBODY'S PERFECT . . ." by Elizabeth C. Gorski
". . . except me!"

ACROSS

1 Robert of "The Sopranos"
5 "Too bad . . ."
9 Lacking hydration
13 Windjammer
17 Fate who spins the thread of life
18 Bordeaux bridge
19 Formula One racer Takuma ___
20 Aust. state
21 In 2007 he homered for the 600th time
23 Winter ammo
25 **Start of a quip**
27 Units named for physicist Nikola
28 Author LeShan and others
29 Plays bass?
33 Carnegie Hall figure
34 Small apts.
35 Head cases?
37 "Toy Story" pig
38 Virility
39 Knack
44 Type of colony Australia was
45 Personality profile info
46 Kane's "Rosebud"
47 Lawmaker of Athens
52 **More of quip**
56 Sights from a cruise ship
57 Pack animals?
58 Tortilla chip topper
59 Emulate Fred Astaire
61 They've got a lot of pull
62 Lack of competence
67 "___ Be In Love": G. Brooks
68 Immature
69 Reveals, in verse
70 "Kyle XY" actress Apanowicz
75 President Sarkozy's predecessor
76 Green stroke
77 Hutton in "American Gigolo"
78 **End of quip**
82 Piece for Yo-Yo Ma
85 Camel in a pack
86 Garfield's pal
87 David Bowie's model wife
88 Joseph Conrad's "___ of Six"
89 Condo owner's bill
90 Roy Orbison's "___ Dooby"
91 Part of ASCII
92 Brit. companies
93 Family tree figures

DOWN

1 Unmoved
2 Bakery sales
3 Tangle, as in a net
4 Promenade
5 Cathedral recesses
6 Kook
7 "I'm waiting for a response . . ."
8 Budding actor's dream
9 Small groups?
10 Called
11 Langston Hughes poem
12 Ruin
13 Skips the night on the town
14 Prince of Broadway
15 Wight or Man: Abbr.
16 J. Major et al.
22 Anniversary unit
24 Russian pancakes
26 Gp. formed in 1948
30 Color shade
31 German border river
32 Steam heat sound
34 Nasser's successor
35 D. Parton's music genre
36 Biology text subj.
37 People of Rwanda
38 Swim team events
39 Madonna's "Take ___"
40 "If you like ___ coladas . . ."
41 Tick's counterpart
42 Bardot's brainstorm
43 File extensions
44 Ford ID
46 Fly-by-night
47 Clean the deck
48 "This can't be!"
49 Mythical mother of twins
50 "Put a lid ___!"
51 Schnapps shots
53 Country singer Travis
54 Neighbors
55 Mariposa lily variety
59 Relating to sugar
60 Dogpatch adjective
61 Chubby Checker song
62 CEO's employer
63 Japanese musical drama
64 Singer DiFranco
65 Fashion designer Luella
66 Coeur d'Alene locale
67 Type of illusion
69 Rank beginner?
70 Bryn ___ College
71 Money of ancient Rome
72 Hawaiian cave
73 Tooth bone
74 Heavenly bodies?
76 Talking point?
77 Juristic exams
79 Man of Pisa
80 Pleased as punch
81 Like fine wine
82 Bill's partner
83 Shogun's capital
84 Ad add-on

153 JAYWALKING by Fred Piscop
4 Down is an example of a riddle clue.

ACROSS

1 They're blind, to bleacher bums
5 Turnstile feature
9 Dickensian epithet
12 Graph line
16 USB connection
17 Popular aerobic program
18 Menu term
19 Catch a Greyhound
20 Canine martial arts expert?
22 "Cabaret" director
24 Played over
25 WW2 meal
27 "I haven't got it ___!"
29 Disney mermaid
31 Surveyor's aid
35 ___ Friday's (restaurant)
36 Astrological sign of some Oslo natives?
40 LL Cool J's "All I Have" partner
41 Place to turn in
42 River through Hesse
43 Deejay's wear
45 Houlihan's rank: Abbr.
46 Do Chisanbop
47 Eastern wrap
50 Janet in "Psycho"
51 Game similar to euchre
53 Dallas bowl
55 Unagi, at the sushi bar
56 Ricky player
57 Waterway allowing some leakage?
60 Scissors beater
63 Suffix with social
65 Latest word
66 Craps natural
68 Charades player
70 Flapper Betty
71 Absorbed, as a loss
72 Shogun's capital
73 "Hanging chads" state
75 Male: Comb. form
77 Swerve at sea
78 "When oysters ___ season"
79 Singer that passes mustard?
83 Workplaces for RN's
84 Farmer's device
86 Cretan capital, formerly
87 Great work
89 Rio beach of song
91 Denis of "Rescue Me"
94 "Hero" singer Enrique
97 The return of Borg?
102 Medieval defense
103 Fighting Tigers' sch.
104 Slowly, on scores
105 Bamako's land
106 Boston orchestra
107 Chucklehead
108 Upper hand
109 Dixie pronoun

DOWN

1 Big Brown
2 Comfy shoe
3 Old hand
4 It has an eye but cannot see
5 Thompson of "Pollock"
6 Foe of Hearns and Hagler
7 Sentence part: Abbr.
8 Withstood hardship
9 Arnaz signature tune
10 Jillions
11 Bar regular
12 Rice-___
13 Letters after nus
14 Check-cashing needs
15 Take a tour of
17 Norse war god
21 It may be used in frying
23 Sign on a lawn
26 Stephen of "Citizen X"
27 Pianist Paderewski
28 Japanese singer with a killer voice?
30 Vitamin qty.
32 Ode to nightwear?
33 Designer to Jackie
34 "The lady ___ protest . . ."
35 Like track events
37 Realm of Herod
38 Moth-eaten
39 Lorelei's river
44 Name on an 84 Across
47 Bra part
48 Toiling away
49 Knock about
52 Choir's place
53 Mob bigwig
54 Word on a dollar
58 Confederate general Early
59 In again
61 Trees of Lebanon
62 Has down
64 Elbow straightener
67 "Il Trovatore" heroine
68 Producers: Abbr.
69 "Would ___?"
71 Modifying wd.
74 Knocks off track
75 Gator tail?
76 "Soul Food" actress
80 Gets slick
81 Skater Naomi Nari
82 Give power to
85 Loses on purpose?
88 Miniature
90 Von Braun's org.
92 De Tirtoff's alias
93 "It's ___-brainer!"
94 Sitter's handful
95 Icky stuff
96 Pool unit
98 Elly May's pa
99 Rte. recommenders
100 Off one's feed
101 Zip

ACROSS

1 Joanna of "Growing Pains"
6 Sink feature
11 Howard on "The Andy Griffith Show"
18 Cause winter travel impairment
19 "No you're not!" retort
20 Falling (over)
21 **Observation: Part I**
23 Actor Robinson
24 Puts up with
25 Actress Aulin
26 Seine specks
27 Bjorn opponent
28 1927 Ford
31 Scat syllable
32 **Observation: Part II**
36 Schnozzle
38 "A Dog of Flanders" author
39 Pale violet
40 Middle name in Memphis
41 Go up against
43 Evasive center?
45 Did a fall chore
46 Dolt
47 Rickey of baseball
49 Bob bit?
51 **Observation: Part III**
56 Met, say
57 Token of victory
58 Frequently, to yeats
61 Ebbing and flowing
64 Word after legal or medical
67 Quintillionth: Prefix
68 PC command
69 Lake near Syracuse
71 Pub lights
73 Headliner's cue
74 **Observation: Part IV**
78 Writer Rosten
79 Vet helper
80 Nobelist Morrison
81 Reason for detention, maybe
83 Account
84 Unsuitably applied handles

89 Made of certain twigs
91 **Observation: Part IV**
93 Inhabiting mountainous regions
94 "I'd like to see ___" (diner's words)
95 Gage title
96 Holds one's interest
97 Breakfast strip
98 Units of force

DOWN

1 Singer Eartha
2 Audio problem
3 Not walk a straight line
4 Club for a pitch
5 Show hostility toward
6 Tried to lose
7 Singer-actress Martha
8 John of "Roots"
9 Pocatello sch.
10 Here–there connector
11 Barbecue stick
12 Propelled a Schwinn
13 VCR remote button
14 Literally, "merry," in Basque
15 Chick flick chat?
16 Be at the heart of
17 Dish discussed in "What's Up, Tiger Lily?"
22 Primary
25 Collections of Scandinavian myths
28 CDVI + DXCVI
29 Ye ___ Antique Shoppe
30 State of mayhem
32 Dotty
33 A dazed boxer may hear it

34 Starsky's partner
35 Khan of R&B
36 Brazil saint
37 Depression agcy.
41 R&B singer India.___
42 Iraqi seaport
44 Went out?
47 Starkville mascot
48 In a lather (with "up")
50 Galba's successor
52 Walking ___ (ecstatic)
53 Malaysian swinger
54 "I beg to differ!"
55 "Kemo sabe" utterer
59 New Deal monogram
60 Abnormally
61 Laborious
62 Like strawberries in the spring
63 Asking questions of, in a way

65 Standing to lose a bundle
66 Hollow
68 Hardly prompt
70 Chisholm Trail stop
72 Olive not meant for martinis
73 Didn't heed
75 Dwellings
76 Why many love crossword solving
77 Prohibition
82 ___ good example
84 Not much time: Abbr.
85 Pay–mind link
86 All tied
87 Cubist painter Magritte
88 Indian titles
90 Duster
91 Origin of Frankenstein's monster
92 Org. with a highly regarded journal